"Eddie Smith is trustworthy, honorable, honest, and competent. He's a clear thinker and a persuasive communicator. When Eddie Smith writes, I read carefully, knowing that he's saying something that will help us all grow."

—Ted Haggard
President, National Association of Evangelicals

"What impresses me about Eddie Smith is his heart for Jesus Christ and his fervent desire to see spiritual awakening happen in our time. An accomplished author and speaker, Eddie has helped promote a movement to incorporate prayer and fasting into the lives of thousands. Through his teachings, as director of PrayUSA!, and his ministry with his wife, Alice, he has helped many walk more deeply with our Lord."

—Steve Douglass
Campus Crusade for Christ

"Eddie Smith has a heart for God and a special concern in the area of prayer. He spoke at three Prayer and Fasting conferences and has played a vital role in the National Prayer Committee. As director of PrayUSA! he has been very effective in mobilizing prayer and fasting for spiritual awakening in our nation and the world."

—Vonette Z. Bright
Cofounder, Campus Crusade for Christ

"Eddie Smith is one of those rare individuals whose life truly touches the heart of God. He is a personal friend, a man of integrity, and one of the reasons America still has a future and a hope."

—Francis Frangipane
Senior minister, River of Life Ministries; author

BREAKING
THE
ENEMY's
GRIP

EDDIE SMITH

BETHANY HOUSE PUBLISHERS
Minneapolis, Minnesota

Published by Bethany House Publishers
11400 Hampshire Avenue South
Bloomington, Minnesota 55438

Bethany House Publishers is a division of
Baker Publishing Group, Grand Rapids, Michigan.

Printed in the United States of America

Library of Congress Cataloging-in-Publication Data

Smith, Eddie.
    Breaking the enemy's grip / by Eddie Smith.
       p.   cm.
    ISBN 0-7642-2998-2 (pbk.)
    1. Spiritual warfare. 2. Spiritual—Christianity. I. Title.

    BV4509.5.S625   2004
    248.4—dc22   2004012905

DEDICATION

Through more than forty years of ministry, no man has impacted my life for Christ more than my own father, Dr. Robert E. Smith. I could tell you of his decades as a businessman, pastor, seminary professor, missionary, school president, and denominational servant. However, none of those things compares with his godly character, his unswerving commitment to the gospel, and his faithfulness to his wife and his Lord Jesus!

Jeff, Tim (my brothers), and I are challenged each day by the example our father continues to live before us. Dad, we thank you! And I lovingly dedicate this book to you.

ABOUT THE AUTHOR

EDDIE SMITH is the cofounder and president of the U.S. Prayer Center, a cross-denominational prayer leader and teacher, an internationally known conference speaker, and an author. Before founding the U.S. Prayer Center in 1990, Eddie and his wife, Alice, served sixteen years in itinerant evangelism and fourteen years in local churches. Eddie and Alice make their home in Houston, Texas.

CONTENTS

CHAPTER ONE

The Adventure Begins

WHAT PRICE FREEDOM?

Horrifically, Aron Ralston had no choice but to amputate his own arm. The twenty-seven-year-old Colorado resident was climbing in Blue John Canyon, adjacent to Canyonlands National Park in southwestern Utah, when a thousand-pound boulder fell on him. His arm was pinned, and he couldn't move for five days. Finally he ran out of water; as one more day passed, he knew that if he wanted to stay alive he had to do something drastic.

The Associated Press reported that Aron used his pocket-knife to amputate his arm below the elbow, then applied a tourniquet and administered first aid. He rigged anchors, fixed a rope, and rappelled seventy feet to the canyon floor. He was hiking downstream to safety when searchers in a helicopter found him. They'd started looking after his employer reported him missing.

One of the rescuers, Sergeant Mitch Vetere, said on the
Today *show that Ralston had no other options if he wanted to*
survive. Had he stayed trapped under the boulder, they never
would have seen him from the air.

The next day rescuers returned to the site to attempt
retrieval of the arm, but they were unable to lift the boulder.
Authorities said that Ralston is an experienced hiker who has
climbed forty-nine of Colorado's major peaks. "I've never seen
anybody who has the will to live and is as much of a warrior as
Aron is, and I've been doing this for twenty-five years," said
park ranger Steve Swanke, who was with Ralston in the emer-
gency room. "He is a warrior—period."[1]

Who would deny that Aron Ralston wanted to be free? It
took great courage and personal sacrifice to get out from
under that rock. Some Christians live—or should I say, they
labor—under a *spiritual* boulder every hour of every day. Either
they don't know how or are simply unwilling to make the
sacrifice necessary for freedom. They are eternally saved from
their sins, but they are not yet spiritually free and victorious
in Christ.

Are you ever plagued by past sin? Although you know that
God has forgiven you, do you sometimes find yourself struggling with guilt about it? If so, you are not alone; I constantly
meet Christians around the world who are experiencing the
same thing. That's why I'm writing this book. And I have
good news for you: There is hope! You don't have to live the
rest of your life under this load.

The very fact that you're reading this book today is proof
that your past sins haven't destroyed you. You've likely experienced enough of Satan's promises to be convinced that none
of them is worthwhile. When it comes to the devil's offers,
there's simply nothing good to go back to, is there? Those
awful things in our past should make us grateful for God's

goodness and for the gracious salvation He offers us in Christ. Before we even begin this journey toward freedom together, I assure you: You can go to bed tonight with a peaceful mind. You can experience a peace that neither money nor medication can give you. This is a peace that comes only from Jesus, the Prince of Peace. To receive it, you must truly trust Him.

MY STORY

In the early 1970s I was minister of music at a wonderful church in the Dallas area. We had doubled in size in two years. People drove from all over the DFW metroplex for services. God showed up regularly. We had a large choir and were producing a music album at the time.

Prior to accepting the job, my wife, Alice, and I had traveled for many years conducting music in churches and stadiums with some of America's best-known crusade evangelists. By then we had produced ten albums, including one with the London Westminster Sinfonia. We had experienced a measure of success; we had lots of things going for us that people dream of and strive for, things we didn't deserve. Some were from God; others, I'm sure, we forged in our own furnace. Of course, we thought we were doing all these things for God, but looking back now, we had mixed motives—some of our religious activity was for ourselves. (I'm amazed at God's patience and love. Aren't you?) I thought we had it all together; at least it seemed everything was going our way.

Then one day the Lord began to expose *the real me* to me. (How other people see us—how we dress, how we speak, how we act in public—may be influential, but it seldom represents our true selves.) He began to show me that I was not the kind of man others thought I was. Though hardly anyone knew my inner struggle, I came to a crisis point. You see, I had always struggled for every morsel of spiritual food I could find. I often felt stalemated in my Christian life; while it appeared that other believers were marching from victory to victory, I seemed to slide from defeat to defeat. (Two steps forward, three steps back. . . .) The battles that raged in my mind seemed to sabotage even my smallest spiritual successes.

Mental accusations based on past sins plagued me. Some were satanic allegations, while others were self-condemnation and feelings of worthlessness. Fact is, *both* were successful in keeping me mentally and spiritually exasperated. I couldn't overcome these obstacles, so they constantly defeated me. Imagine my surprise when I discovered that neither of them was justified.

Using one Bible teacher after another, book after book, and experience after experience, the Lord disclosed the lies I'd believed. He showed me how I was ignorantly undercutting my own spiritual and mental health. He also revealed to me the means by which the devil was trying to gain victory in my life.

Great news! God disclosed a biblical strategy that so completely set me free that it's been many years since I've had to deal with such mental rubbish. The truth is, He showed me how to live in such a way that any satanic accusation thrown at me is welcome. *Welcome?* Yes. *Why* is it welcome? Odd as it may sound, as a result of implementing this approach, the devil's accusations against me now cost *him* far more than they can possibly cost me. Tens of thousands have also found freedom through this message, and you can as well!

On that liberating day, I sat down under a tree on my front lawn with pen and pad to listen to and to do business with God. The book you are holding in your hand is a result of my encounter with Him that day. I had to *work it out* in order to *walk it out*. I will now provide the tools that can bring you to a fulfilling level of Christian living that many dream about but few discover. *This is the resurrected life God has always meant for you to enjoy.* Before we finish, you are going to need your own pen and pad; for now, let's lay a foundation for our freedom.

(*Note:* If you have never received Christ as your personal Lord and Savior, please turn now to Appendix A. Do not proceed with this book until you've received God's forgiveness for your sins, settled the issue of your eternal destiny, and know for certain that Christ lives in you. The new birth is the launching pad—without it you can never soar the heavenlies!)

DISCOVERY ONE: YOUR NEW FUTURE

One day Jesus told His disciples, "I am come that they [humans] might have life, and that they might have it more abundantly" (John 10:10). A rather strange statement to make to living people, don't you think? Imagine how it must have sounded to them at the time; after all, they already *had* blood flowing through their veins. That's *life,* isn't it?

We, of course, hear Jesus' words with the clarity of an additional two thousand years. We know that although His original hearers were *physically* alive, they were *spiritually* dead, separated from God and His plan by their sins. Jesus had come to bring them spiritual life. He had come to literally give them *His* life so that they could live victoriously on earth and live forever with God in heaven.

Let's investigate, then, the eternal life that Christ has given us.

All life-forms have three things in common: a past, a present, and a future. The moment we (1) acknowledged that Christ's death paid the price for sin; (2) repented of our sins; (3) believed in our hearts that God raised Jesus from the dead; and (4) confessed that He is our Lord,[2] He inexplicably came to live inside us by His Holy Spirit. We actually received Christ's own life—what John referred to as *eternal life,*[3] which is not a quantity but a *quality* of life.

The King James Version of John 3:16 says that those who believe will have "everlasting life." The fact is, the *quantity* of our lives is a settled matter. Although our days on earth are numbered, Scripture is clear that all people will live forever, somewhere.[4] The real question: *Where* will we live forever?

The difference between the *quality* of life for the lost person and the saved person is another matter; quality varies greatly on earth and extraordinarily throughout eternity. The lost on earth are limited to human nature, their natural life source, and then they face eternity in hell, separated from God. *God never intended this*. He created hell as a place of eternal punishment for the devil and his fallen angels.[5] Scripture blatantly declares, however, that lost people—those who have never received God's forgiveness and redemption—are children of the devil, who was the first to reject God.[6] If they reject salvation and die without Christ, they will spend eternity apart from Him.

John 3:16 in the *New International Version* says that we who believe will receive *eternal life*. The triune God alone is eternal; He created everything else for His own pleasure and purposes.[7] So eternal life is God-life—*God's own life*. It is eternal life, God's life within, that distinguishes the saved from the lost. The moment you received Christ, you knew that you had eternal life and that heaven was your ultimate home.[8] We who have received eternal life are equipped to live with God on earth and to live with Him forever in heaven. Heaven is a prepared place for a prepared people.[9] That's *quality* living.

Therefore, the initial revelation that God gives to us as new believers, "babes in Christ,"[10] doesn't pertain to our present state but to our future. We realize, *I'm not going to hell. I'm going to live forever with God in heaven!*

DISCOVERY TWO: YOUR NEW PRESENT

Spiritual maturity requires time—you can't rush it. Many years ago when our oldest son, Robert, was a preschooler, he and I were waiting patiently as his mom shopped for a pair of shoes. He was entertaining himself with the shoehorns, the mirrors, and anything else at hand.

To pass the time, I called him over to where I was seated and, though teasing, asked in a serious tone, "Son, when are you going to grow up?" A puzzled expression fell across his cherubic face. Robert precociously put his tiny index finger to his chin, rolled his big brown eyes, furrowed his little brow, thought for a moment, and answered confidently, "I'm gonna do it right now, Daddy." With that, he stood on his tiptoes, stretched his little shoulders up, craned his neck, and strained with all his might. He gave it his all, then said with a look of resignation, "Daddy, I'm gonna let myself do it."

Just as Robert couldn't physically grow up that day, you can't grow into spiritual maturity today: There are simply no shortcuts to spiritual adulthood. And spiritual maturity is not to be confused with *living the Spirit-filled life*[11] or with *exercising spiritual gifts;*[12] both of these are possible for a brand-new Christian. *Spiritual maturity* is an entirely different matter.

About thirty years ago in Dallas, a young man came to Christ in our church. B. J. was fresh off the streets and direct from the drug culture, a well-known figure in the community. For the first three weeks after he was saved, I don't think his feet ever touched the ground; he was electrified with his new-found faith. It was fun to watch as he witnessed to everything that moved. If it didn't move, he'd put a gospel tract on it!

Then suddenly B. J. was gone—he absolutely disap-peared. We didn't see him for more than a month. Finally one night he wandered back into our services, looking terrible. At the conclusion, when the invitation was given, he came weeping to the altar, deeply broken and sorrowfully repentant. He told the spellbound congregation of his past life in sin and his remarkable conversion experience. Next he spoke of his new life in Christ and his struggle to live it. Humiliated, he tearfully confessed that he had crashed and burned because of his spiritual pride, summarizing with, "I guess I thought I was *super-saved* or somethin'."

We do baby believers a disservice when we fail to teach them that *spiritual maturity is a gradual journey that entails knowing God's Word and using it to determine good from evil.* The writer of Hebrews explains it this way:

> *For every one that useth milk [is] unskilful in the word of righteousness: for he is a babe. But strong meat belongeth to them that are of full age, even those who by reason of use have their senses exercised to discern both good and evil.* (5:13–14)

A newborn believer who is unfamiliar with the Bible and with hearing the voice of God can only digest "milk"—elementary spiritual truths. However, a seasoned Christian, who has applied the Word and the Voice to real-life experiences over the years, is better able to discern right from wrong and capable of processing "strong meat."

Each person's spiritual growth is individually governed and guided by God himself. It takes years to produce a towering oak tree, but only a few months to produce a squash. Accordingly, unless you want to become a spiritual squash, don't rush the process!

In time we move beyond the initial revelation of our heavenly *future* and begin to realize that Christ didn't save us just so that we could *live for Him.* He actually saved us so that He could *live His life in us,* right now, present tense![13]

God created everything that exists for His own glory, including us.[14] Everything He does on earth is for His glory, and He commands that we also bring glory to Him.[15] Christ does not live in us simply to assure us of missing hell and making heaven—He wants to glorify himself through us *now,* in the present.[16] Along the way, in the natural process of our growth in Him, we begin to focus less on our ultimate future and more on our immediate present—the amazing here and now. We are challenged with the eternal potential of our present spiritual experiences.

God intends to live His own life in our earthly bodies, and Christ wants to reign in and through us. The requirement for this is sobering: We are to do *nothing* to exalt ourselves so that He can be *everything* in us.[17] We are to die to our carnal nature in order to live out His holy life.[18] Gradually, with the aid of our two earthly teachers (our mentors and our mistakes) and our heavenly teacher (the Holy Spirit), we learn that Christ is to be our life.[19] Through our daily surrender, by confessing and turning from sin, presenting God with clean and empty vessels (our lives) for Him to fill with His Spirit, He makes himself at home in us. Not only do we look forward to our future in heaven with Him, but eternity has now invaded our physical bodies (our "earthsuits") and Christ has become our very existence.[20]

So how does this play out in a practical sense? To illustrate, suppose there was going to be a golf tournament in Houston next week—say, the Lone Star Open—and that the winner would receive a one-million-dollar prize. Now, I'm no golfer; I've only played two or three rounds in my entire life, and all I really accomplished was to lose all the golf balls I could afford and anger every other player in my foursome. Alice even beats me at miniature golf!

However, suppose I knew a way to conjure up the spirit of the great and long-departed golfing legend Ben Hogan. Imagine that I could invite Ben's spirit to come inside my body. (I know it's weird, but bear with me and you'll get the point . . . I hope.)

I would arrive to play with Tiger Woods, Ernie Els, Vijay Singh, and the game's other greats. With today's flawless equipment *and* with Hogan's near-perfect accuracy, I would split every fairway, strike short irons with ease, miss every hazard, hit every green, putt with nerves of steel, and birdie hole after hole. The world's best players would be amazed that I, an unknown rookie, could have such skill and courage.

But it wouldn't have been me who won the prize at all. It would have been the magnificent Ben Hogan, simply doing it through me. In a similar way, the Holy Spirit (Christ *in us*) glorifies God the Father as He lives His life through us, which is our ultimate purpose and calling.

DISCOVERY THREE: YOUR NEW PAST

The final phase of our spiritual discovery has to do with a new revelation of our *past*. Remember, every life-form has a past, a present, and a future. Our future is in heaven with God, and our present is Christ in us, which is how we glorify God on this earth. But the most mystifying of these divine revelations concerns our past. Since Christ is our new life, our old life has been replaced—its future in hell is no more, its present (fleshly living) is to be brought under the Spirit's control, and its dark past is made new by the finished work of Jesus, our Light.[21]

That's right: The Christ-life we received at the point of our salvation comes to us complete with its own past:[22] We are complete in Jesus! Amazingly, we learn that when Christ died on Calvary's cross, we died in Him, and that when He was raised, we were raised in Him.[23] Paul exhorts, "Since, then, you have been raised with Christ, set your hearts on things above, where Christ is seated at the right hand of God" (Colossians 3:1 NIV).

A generation ago my dear friend the late Dr. R. G. Lee was known as "the prince of preachers." For thirty-two years he was pastor of Bellevue Baptist Church in Memphis. He was also famous for his sermon "Payday Someday," a convincing and dramatic portrayal of the story of Ahab and Jezebel that depicted the inevitable consequences of unrepented sin.

One morning while on a Holy Land tour in Jerusalem, as Dr. Lee exited the garden tomb, the guide asked him, "Dr. Lee, have you been inside this tomb before?" Dr. Lee smiled and replied, "Yes, son, I walked out of here nearly two thousand years ago!"

Mysteriously, God placed us *in Christ* before the foundations of the world;[24] this is the nature of the *eternal life* in us. Therefore, you need not be driven by the weaknesses of your own past; now you must draw your strength from His.[25] The ancestral sins, generational iniquities, and deep-seated weaknesses of your forefathers need not hinder you from fully reaching your kingdom potential.

In this book I'll be showing you how to be free from these maladies. The guilt of your past sin need not torment you. It's entirely possible to remember your past, even the offenses committed against you, and experience no emotional distress at all. In fact, those things can become monuments of God's grace in your life. You are an entirely *new creation,* with a new future, a new present, and even a new past.[26] Is this great, or what?!

It occurs to me that you might ask, "Does every Christian have to take the steps you outline in this book in order to live freely and be godly?" The answer is no. For various reasons, many Christians live successfully without ever specifically addressing some of these issues.

1. Each of us has a different family and personal history; we each enter our Christian experience with different "spiritual baggage." The process of maturing in Christ can include putting away these things, whatever they might be for each person.

2. While Christ's atoning work is completely finished, having given us the opportunity to become new creatures and

live a new life in Him, *the existence of* and *our experience of* those finished blessings are different matters. Someone depositing a million dollars in your checking account is one thing; your knowing how to write and cash checks is another.

3. Christ's cross-work was a *legal* (judicial) matter. Satan, God's archenemy, is the ultimate outlaw, meaning he is lawless and therefore has no regard for legal stipulations. One future day he'll no longer have that choice—for he will be once-and-for-all cast into hell's lake of fire. But for now, working with Satan is our lower nature—our flesh—which God allows to coexist within us, even after our justification, to teach us to overcome. Each of us must deal with satanic accusation, self-condemnation, temptations, and tendencies to certain sins, even though we've been born again.

Therefore, I have written *Breaking the Enemy's Grip* to help you learn to "cash the checks" that will enable you to quench Satan's fiery darts,[27] to deal a daily death-blow to your flesh nature just as the apostle Paul "died daily,"[28] and to experience more of what Christ has sacrificially earned on your behalf. I implore you: Devour it!

CHAPTER TWO

Mission Impossible!

You may be asking, "If the Christian life is this wonderful, then why am I having such a hard time living it?" Friend, living the Christian life isn't difficult at all: *It's mission impossible!* That's right. In the same way that you cannot live the Eddie Smith life, or I live your life, neither of us can live Christ's life. The good news is that contrary to what many people think, *God never meant for us to live the Christian life.*

Remember, Jesus is alive, and He's alive for a reason: He has chosen to live *His life,* by His Spirit's presence, in us who believe! However, there is a rub. Actually there are three rubs—the world, the flesh, and the devil. Thankfully, we are not left on the battlefield of life wondering who or what is our enemy:

- *the world system,* which still languishes under the curse of sin;
- *the flesh,* our human nature (our natural state, without Christ); and

- *Satan,* a fallen angel whose highest priority is to be worshiped as God.[1]

These are the enemies of the Christ-life that God desires to produce in us. And we can neither crucify the devil nor cast out the flesh (ours or others'). Precise weaponry is required for us to overcome each of these opponents.

Late one night I was witnessing with Jim, another evangelist, in a South Texas bar. Jim began sharing Christ with a huge, hairy, and obviously disinterested man, who unexpectedly jumped to his feet, grabbed Jim by the throat, and screamed, "If you mention the name *Jesus* one more time, I'm gonna cut your heart out!" At this, Jim pointed his finger in the giant's face and said sternly, "I bind you in the name of Jesus!" For a moment both seemed frozen in a standoff, so I solicitously stepped between them and cautioned, "Jim, if this is a demon, you might be able to bind it. If this is his flesh, he's gonna kill you!" (By the way, it *was* his flesh.)

To defeat and escape the snare of the world system, we must identify its lies, die to its appeal, and focus our attention and affection upon our gracious God.[2] To defeat the desires of the flesh, we must refuse to acknowledge or accommodate it. More than that, we are to literally run away from lustful temptations.[3] Bottom line: We must stop giving our flesh what it wants by no longer yielding to its demands.

My wife, Alice, is a compassionate animal lover. If she had her way, we would put out food for every stray dog and cat in the neighborhood. If we did that, though, we would be quickly overrun with animals—feed one hungry appetite, and you feed them all.

The same is true of our flesh, which thrives on the lusts of this world. This fallen world system is designed to entice our flesh to sin, and our flesh is in cahoots with this fallen world system. If we embrace the world's ways, our flesh will continue to rule us. Even *common sense* would tell the person with a chemical addiction (e.g., alcohol or nicotine) to stay away from other users if he wants to quit. But we who are in Christ actually possess an *uncommon sense:* We have the mind of *Christ!*[4]

If we routinely feed our flesh a little here and a little there, it will eventually consume us. Again, that's why God warns us to "flee also youthful lusts."[5] Instead of feeding our flesh, we are to reckon it dead so that Christ (and not our flesh-nature) will be our life source.

TEMPTATION ISN'T SIN

Strangely, while some Christians are defeated because they refuse to take responsibility for things that *are* their responsibility, others are defeated because they choose to take responsibility for things that *aren't.* To reckon your flesh dead, you must *stop owning its activity.* For example, it may surprise you to learn that you are not accountable for all your thoughts. Although the enemy can't read your mind, he can certainly put thoughts there.

Joan came to me for counseling one day, broken and humiliated over a sordid erotic dream she'd had the night before. When she began sharing with me the revolting specifics, I gently interrupted her. "Joan, you don't have to share those details with me.[6] The only question I have is, what have you done about the dream?"

"As soon as I awoke from this awful nightmare, I fell out of bed and onto my face and repented to the Lord for it," she said.

"Why did you repent for a dream over which you had no control? If my doorbell rang right now and I opened the door to find a delivery man with twelve pizzas in his arms asking me for $143, I wouldn't pay him. *I haven't ordered any pizza!* You didn't order that dream, did you?"

"Well, no. Of course I didn't."

"Then, Joan," I continued, "what are you doing paying for it by repenting? There is nothing for which you should repent. You didn't sin. There is no guilt! This is simply another of the devil's ways of falsely accusing you."

James wrote, "Therefore to him that knoweth to do good, and doeth it not, to him it is sin" (James 4:17). We are responsible for *our choices*. Sometimes random evil thoughts do enter our minds. Haven't you noticed how often this happens the moment you begin to study the Word or start to pray? At that moment you face a choice: You can either evict that disgusting thought, or you can pull up a chair and invite the nasty thing to stay. Joan went home with a liberating revelation.

King David didn't sin because he *saw* Bathsheba bathing; there's a difference between what you *see* and what you *look* at. Sin is a matter of the will. When David saw Bathsheba, he should have turned and walked away. Sadly, he did not, and, in hindsight, the road to his sin is quite clear: He *looked,* he *lingered,* he *lusted,* and he eventually *lay* with her. I often say, "We are not necessarily responsible for our thoughts, but we *are* responsible for our thinking." David's poignant words carry particular meaning: "Let the words of my mouth, and *the meditation of my heart*, be acceptable in thy sight, O LORD, my strength, and my redeemer" (Psalm 19:14, emphasis added).

While Satan is God's enemy, it's highly unlikely that he knows your name. Why would you think he does? He is neither omniscient, omnipotent, nor omnipresent; like us, he has limited knowledge, he has limited power, and he can only be one place at a time. There are already more than six billion people on this planet!

Nevertheless, he has lived for many, many years—at one point in the very presence of the Lord—and some assume that he can travel at the speed of light.[7] He is certainly supported by a multitude of organized fallen angels and/or evil spirits who were cast out of heaven with him.[8] So he *is* a formidable foe.

But in all likelihood, Satan himself will never know our names. We will probably never personally encounter him as Jesus did. Even so, we will constantly confront his evil minions as long as we live. Thus, when we speak of "the devil," we are sometimes referring to his entire depraved kingdom.

So how do we deal with the devil? To defeat the devil, *we must learn the truth*. Satan is the father of lies and was a liar from the beginning.[9] So are his companion spirits. Therefore, we overcome his system with truth. When Satan confronted Jesus in the wilderness, Jesus answered each of his attacks with Scripture, the Word of Truth.[10] Satan could not find a place in Christ, because since childhood He had studied the Scriptures. In fact, when He was only twelve years old, Jesus was found one day in the temple teaching the teachers![11]

THE DILEMMA

Many believers are happy that they're saved but not saved enough to be happy. They walk with one foot in darkness and the other in the light. Rather than marching from victory unto victory, they drag from one defeat to the next. They straddle the fence and continually struggle to live up to their kingdom potential. In their wake lies one failed good intention after another.

Paul explained his dilemma in bewildering terms with which we can all identify:

For that which I do I allow not: for what I would, that do I not; but what I hate, that do I. If then I do that which I would not, I consent unto the law that it is good. Now then it is no more I that do it, but sin that dwelleth in me. For I know that in me (that is, in my flesh,) dwelleth no good thing: for to will is present with me; but how to perform that which is good I find not. For the good that I would I do not: but the evil which I would not, that I do. Now if I do that I would not, it is no more I that do it, but sin that dwelleth in me. I find then a law, that, when I would do good, evil is present with me. For I delight in the law of God after the inward man: But I see another law in my members, warring against the law of my mind, and bringing me into captivity to the law of sin which is in my members. O wretched man that I am! who shall deliver me from the body of this death? (Romans 7:15–24)

Many believers know that they have been born again, that heaven is their home, and that they are new creations in Christ. However, this truth isn't evidenced in their day-to-day experience. Some Christians are bound with addictions, some have little or no self-control, some are mentally or emotionally tormented, and many feel spiritually stuck. In their minds they know the truth, but the truth has not yet set them free. If their condition frustrates them, can you imagine how saddened Christ must be? After all, He's the one who should be living in and through them!

Through intimidation and accusation, Satan hinders us from going on with God. He loves to remind us of our past sins, even those we committed before we came to Christ. Maybe you're thinking, *Hasn't God forgiven those sins and removed my guilt?* Sure He has. But Satan couldn't care less about what God has done. Satan is trying to denigrate the blood of Jesus; to him, all's fair in love and war . . . and this is war. Satan is fighting for his reputation. Stealing, killing, and destruction are his modus operandi.

It's not surprising that the Bible identifies Satan as the "accuser of the brethren" (Revelation 12:10). The following story, told by Martin Luther, clarifies an important point:

> Once upon a time, the devil came to me, and said, "Martin Luther, you are a great sinner and you will be damned."
>
> "Stop! Stop!" said I, "one thing at a time. I am a great sinner, that is true, though you have no right to tell me of it. I confess it. What next? 'Therefore you will be damned.' That is not good reasoning. It is true that I am a great sinner; but it is written, 'Jesus came to save sinners'; and therefore I shall be saved."
>
> So I cut the devil off with his own sword; and he went away mourning, because he could not cast me down by calling me a sinner.[12]

Along with satanic accusation, we wrestle with self-condemnation—that's right, *self*-condemnation. Ridiculous, isn't it? We can easily become our own worst enemy. And self-condemnation can be even more devastating to a sincere Christian than satanic accusation. Why? Because it is sometimes easier for us to identify Satan's lies than to spot our own! Why is Satan so effective at luring us into condemning ourselves? There are several reasons.

1. *Our sense of justice can keep us self-condemned.* God has created us in His image. Deep inside we are programmed to demand justice: Sinners should be punished, and our consciences demand punishment. Without a full revelatory knowledge of Christ's payment for their sin, some Christians confess and re-confess and never realize reconciliation with God . . . even though they *are* reconciled to Him through the shed blood of Jesus.

2. *Our inability to shed guilt even though we have received God's*

forgiveness and cleansing through the blood of Jesus. We can *be* forgiven but still *feel* guilty. If we feel guilty, we cannot enjoy the forgiveness of Romans 8:1: "There is therefore now no condemnation to them which are in Christ Jesus." If we can't enjoy the result of being reconciled with God, we can't effectively minister it to others: "God, who hath reconciled us to himself by Jesus Christ . . . hath given to us the ministry of reconciliation" (2 Corinthians 5:18).

3. *Our ignorance of what God has done for us often neutralizes us.* For you to have inherited one million dollars will mean nothing to you unless you *know* it. For example, a child king will never learn the full benefits, authority, and power he wields until he reaches adulthood. Again, Jesus taught in John 8:32, "Ye shall know the truth, and the truth shall make you free." Notice, it's not just the truth that makes us free; it's *knowing* the truth. The truth must be revealed, believed, and known in order to be experienced.

Here are several things we must *know* in order to experience freedom from satanic intimidation.

- God forgives and cleanses us! ("[He] forgiveth all thine iniquities" [Psalm 103:3]; "If we confess our sins, He is faithful and just . . . to cleanse us from all unrighteousness" [1 John 1:9].)
- God removes our sin and redeems us! ("As far as the east is from the west, so far hath He removed our transgressions from us" [Psalm 103:12]; "I have blotted out, as a thick cloud, thy transgressions, and, as a cloud, thy sins: return unto me; for I have redeemed thee" [Isaiah 44:22].)
- God forgets our sins and buries them in the depths of the sea! ("I will forgive their iniquity, and I will remember their sin no more" [Jeremiah 31:34]; "Thou wilt cast all their sins into the depths of the sea" [Micah 7:19].)

As long as we are ignorant of these truths, we will be easy

targets for the enemy's intimidation. Rather than enjoying our relationship with God, we will continually question it.

4. Finally, *we fall prey to satanic accusation and self-condemnation when we have never fully declared our independence from the kingdom of darkness.* Although we have received salvation, forgiveness, and cleansing, we must specifically break off our old relationship with Satan.

In Acts 19 we find an example of this. The Ephesian Christians severed all ties with their past when they burned the occult books and artifacts that related to their former lives. Many of God's people today have never taken back the ground they've given the enemy. Christians naïvely assume that Satan will either willingly accept or be forced to accept that they now belong to God. This is not the case! Satan loves to spiritually cripple believers with unwanted and unwarranted reminders of sins they committed before salvation. Because of this, we may still struggle with false guilt over those sins we've confessed, from which we've repented and been cleansed and forgiven. Let's see if we can get a handle on this in the next chapter.

CHAPTER THREE

Four Stages of Christian Living

Bill and Mary had been married for many years. Their kids, now grown, no longer lived at home. Mary was a committed Christian, but Bill was not. His life had always revolved around his business.

Mary's church was conducting an evangelistic crusade, and she convinced Bill to attend the final Sunday evening service with her. To make him more comfortable, they sat near the back of the auditorium. As the evangelist finished preaching his gospel message, he offered an invitation for people to come and receive Christ. Bill began to experience God's convicting power. Overwhelmed with the guilt of his sin, he tearfully stepped into the aisle and stumbled his way to the altar. There he confessed his sin, repented, and invited Jesus to be the Lord of his life. Bill was wonderfully saved, and both he and Mary were ecstatic.

Later that night they were almost asleep when Bill's heart was suddenly gripped by fear and guilt. He tried to shake it, but he couldn't. Choking back tears he said, "Mary, honey, I love you. But I have something I need to confess to you."

"Is it about Janet?" Mary asked.

"Yes," Bill shuddered. "But how do you know about Janet?"

"Bill, I've known about your affair for two years."

Utterly ashamed, Bill asked, "Mary, could you ever find it in your heart to forgive me?"

She smiled, caressed his chin in her hand, and said, "Sweetheart, tonight God forgave all of your sins. Of course I forgive you." They peacefully fell asleep.

———————

The next day Bill left for work. He was born again—everything was fresh! On his way home he picked up flowers for Mary; he could hardly believe the warmth of their Christ-centered relationship. "Why did I wait so long?" he asked himself.

Tuesday morning, Bill called home and invited Mary to meet him for lunch at their favorite restaurant. They felt newly wed.

Midmorning on Wednesday, Bill was interrupted by his secretary's voice. "Bill," she announced abruptly over the intercom, "Janet is here to see you."

His blood turned to ice water. No! Not Janet, not now! Then it dawned on him: He'd made everything right with God, and he'd made everything right with Mary, but he'd forgotten to break off his relationship with Janet. Janet was simply operating according to the knowledge she had.[1]

Many Christians are like Bill. They've made everything right with God and with others, but they haven't known how to break off their relationship with sin and with Satan's kingdom. Rather than living as overcomers, they are unnecessarily being defeated in some areas of their lives, ruled by uncontrolled sins and harmful attitudes. Worldly distractions discourage them from God's ways. When they should be sitting at the table with Christ, their Bridegroom, feasting as Ruth did,[2] they're gleaning in the fields, living off the leftovers.[3] Many are living less like the spiritually wealthy bride of Christ and more like spiritually impoverished widows who struggle to get by. They're living compromised Christian lives rather than the resurrected Christ-life. They've yet to discover that *deliverance is the children's bread;*[4] freedom in Christ is their inheritance. Does this sound like you? If so, then fasten your seat belt—I have great news!

Our journey has four stages, through which each of us moves at a different pace. These stages can clearly be seen in four major events in the Old Testament experienced by the children of Israel. Let's look at them together.

Stage One: The Passover (Exodus 13)

The first Passover was a celebration of Israel's exodus from four hundred years of Egyptian bondage. According to the Lord's instructions, they applied lamb's blood to the beams and doorposts of their homes, thereby diverting the death angel. The Passover is symbolic of our *salvation,* the first stage of our Christian experience. By the application of the blood of the Lamb (Jesus) upon our lives, our own spiritual death is averted and we are born again—set free from bondage to Satan and given the gift of eternal life.

Stage Two: The Red Sea Crossing (Exodus 14)

Their second powerful experience was crossing the Red Sea. We will later return to deal with this in more detail.

Stage Three: The Wilderness Wandering (Exodus 15–Joshua 2)

The third Israelite experience that parallels our Christian lives is their wilderness wandering. For forty years God's people wandered in the desert. When the twelve spies returned from the Promised Land with reports of the bounty that lay ahead of them, the tired and discouraged Israelites had an opportunity to leave the desert. But because of fear and unbelief, they would not, and they were forced to continue their desert sojourn.

Israel's wilderness wandering parallels the *early years* of our Christian walk. It was in the desert that they learned who God is and how He operates, about relationships and how to live under spiritual authority. Even in their childish complaining, they learned of their own sinful proclivities, their internal enemy (their flesh), and the importance of obeying God's law. His provision and protection became an everyday revelation to them as they watched water miraculously gush from a rock and manna mysteriously appear from heaven. It was in the wilderness that their spiritual maturity was developed . . . and the same can be said for us.

Remember: Spiritual maturity, like physical maturity, is a result of *time* and *experiences* through which we have applied God's Word to help us discern good from evil, truth from falsehood.[5] Slip and fall? Sure, we all do from time to time. But we don't stay down! We get up, confess our sin, hold up our heads, and move forward with Christ. After all, without trials, life would have no triumphs. Without tests, we'd have no testimony. If we will let Him, God will turn our messes into a message!

As we walk this journey with Christ, the Lord will challenge our flesh. About the time we think we know something, He will give us an attitude adjustment. Sometimes in our desert wanderings, He will withhold His voice from us to see if we'll stay our course and wait on Him or if we'll run back to our old familiar and destructive sinful habits.

There are times when we (like the Israelites) see the miracles of God and *still* allow pride to creep into our hearts. The Lord has no other alternative than to allow us to fail. These types of experiences are part of our learning how to grow spiritually in Christ. Once again: Life's earthly teachers are our mentors and our mistakes.

Stage Four: The Promised Land (Joshua 3)

The final phase of Israel's journey, which we will consider as it relates to our faith journey, was their entrance into the Promised Land.

It's often taught that crossing the river Jordan is symbolic of death and that entering into the Promised Land represents heaven. Others say that the Promised Land depicts Spirit-filled living. But it was in the Promised Land that the children of Israel began to confront and defeat their enemies. The Promised Land is symbolic of our warfare and victory. The Lord delivered His people through the sea from the hands of Pharaoh. They only had to *obey* Him.

Do you remember the bliss of being newly redeemed? In the early stages of Christian living we simply obeyed our new Master, and He removed the obstacles that would have hindered our progress. But in time, things changed—no longer was life so automatic and predictable. The day came when we began having to confront "the three Ts": *temptation, trial,* and *testing.* We were forced to fight against the enemy of our soul on a daily basis.

In the Promised Land, the Israelites were forced to face and fight their enemies. Why? God's plan required that they move into maturity; they were, as we are, to become overcomers. They had to overcome their internal enemy (the flesh) in the wilderness, and in the Promised Land they had to overcome their external enemies.

DON'T SKIP THE WILDERNESS—YOU'RE GOING TO NEED IT

Listen carefully: One of the problems in the church today is that some are trying to get people who have experienced *the Passover* (salvation) to enter *the Promised Land* (spiritual warfare and victory) before they've ever experienced *the Red Sea Crossing* (separation from sin and the devil) and *the Wilderness Wandering* (dying to self and growth to maturity). Baby Christians are sometimes prematurely moving (or being foolishly led) to the front line of spiritual battle, where many are soundly defeated.

It was forty years before the children of Israel were grounded enough in faith to enter the Promised Land and engage in battle. Not one man or woman who was familiar with Egyptian warfare was even allowed to go there.[6] The generation who faced Pharaoh and his armies died; it was a new generation that couldn't rely on past experience that marched boldly into the Promised Land.

God wasn't looking for warriors like those Pharaoh had commanded. He was looking for a new breed, those who knew their God and would follow never-been-done-before methods of warfare. God was raising up a generation that knew the battle was the Lord's and that He himself would assure the victory.

As long as we think the battle is ours, we will remain defeated. How you dealt with temptation and sin before you found Christ is of no value to you now. In fact, it will actually hinder you. God will not stoop to compete with us and our puny human efforts. Once we tire of our fleshly methods, the Lord will begin to give us the victory!

In the Promised Land, Israel began to advance God's kingdom. It was there that they confronted the "-ites" (the Hittites, the Jebusites, the Canaanites, the Parasites . . . just kidding). In the Promised Land they learned to fight *with* (alongside) the Lord instead of *for* the Lord. The Lord of Hosts doesn't *send* us into battle, He *leads* us into battle.

God will lead you into battle also. Why? Because in battle . . .

- You are made strong.
- You will see demonstrations of the Lord's power.
- God's kingdom will be extended through you.

More than two hundred times in Scripture, our Savior is referred to as the Lord of Hosts or the Lord of heaven's army! The Christian life is ultimately a life of battle.[7] Deal with it.

RETURN TO THE RED SEA CROSSING

Now, as promised, let's take a closer look at what the Red Sea crossing symbolized. Some say it was symbolic of baptism. Not so—they didn't get wet! It wasn't about the water; it was about their enemy: "Because of their faith, the people walked through the Red Sea on dry land; but when the Egyptians tried to do so, they were drowned" (Hebrews 11:29 NIV).

The significance of the Red Sea experience was Israel's deliverance from Pharaoh and his armies. *It is at the Red Sea of our lives that we are freed from the grip of the evil one.* But, once again, we must know the truth in order to be set free.[8]

As mentioned, many Christians who have experienced the Passover (salvation) have not yet been through *the Red Sea* (separation). Like Pharaoh and his armies, Satan and his minions are still on their heels, breathing down their necks, making their lives miserable. Perhaps you also lie awake at night sweating over false guilt. You know that your sin-guilt is removed—Jesus paid it all, right?—and yet you cannot find peace of mind. You continually cry out to God, but what you are crying out for isn't a God issue; it's between you and the evil one. God is not the one who must settle this matter, you are. He has defeated Satan. Now you must live as an over-comer. *It's your move!*

When I was a young boy, I would play checkers with my granddaddy. The only thing I remember him ever saying was, "It's your move." You see, I would move my checker on the board, but while he was thoughtfully determining and making his next move, with my short attention span I would get distracted by other things. Before I knew it, Granddaddy would tap me on the arm, interrupting my daydreams with the words, "It's your move."

Now let's transfer this example to your situation. You've cried out to God about the enemy. You've whined and com-plained. But Satan, the accuser of the brethren, loves the attention you pay him. Something nasty keeps hanging on to you. Paul understood it; in Romans 7:24, at his wits' end, he cried out to God, "O wretched man that I am! Who shall deliver me from the body of this death?"

Following Lazarus's resurrection, Christ instructed his friends to help loose him from his graveclothes; he was still bound, even though he was no longer dead. You *know* you're alive in Christ, but you *feel* at times as though you're spiritu-ally dead. The reason is that although you've experienced *the Passover* (salvation), you haven't yet experienced *the Red Sea* (separation). Your enemies, like Pharaoh and his armies, are still at your heels, pursuing you and generally making your life miserable.

Believe me, when you pass through your Red Sea expe-rience, Satan will no longer intimidate you. In fact, you will intimidate him. Satan won't be accusing you anymore; you'll be accusing him. He'll no longer be attempting to prosecute you in heaven's court; you'll be prosecuting him in heaven's court. He won't be destroying your works; *you'll be destroying his!*

Life is a lot like an automobile: If it has a three-year warranty, it appears to be intentionally manufactured to break down at precisely three years and one day. God has developed the Christian life to bring us to the end of ourselves. On our own, we take one step forward and two steps back . . . one step forward and two steps back. At this pace, we'll never reach God's best for our lives. More precisely, we'll actually be moving in the wrong direction.

If you will discipline yourself to read and follow through with the assignments in this book, you will go through your own Red Sea experience. If you are encamped at the sea today, God has thrown your enemy into confusion. If you don't abort the process, you will soon experience spiritual deliverance on a fresh new level.

Years ago there lived an English widow and her grown son. The son was having difficulty finding employment, when he read in the newspaper about an offer of free land: The Australian government was trying to populate their vast wilderness by offering it free, in sections, to anyone who would clear it, build a home on it, and farm it. The young man thought this was an awesome opportunity.

His application was ultimately approved, so he made plans to leave England and sail to Australia. When the day of his departure finally arrived, he had a heart-to-heart talk with his mother.

"Mother," he said, "I'm going to Australia. But I will write to you every week. And I will see to it that all your needs are met. You will never want for anything. Trust me." With that he kissed her and boarded his ship.

The widow missed her son terribly the first few weeks.

However, she soon returned to her daily routine. And, as promised, every week she received a postcard from him, each with its own beautiful picture of Australian life. The elderly mother would keep the postcards in her purse to remember her son. She especially liked showing them to her friends: "This," she would say with pride, pointing to the picture, "is a Koala bear. They are native to Australia, where my son lives." Soon her purse and Bible were filled with postcards. She decided to display them in her home, on the wall of her hallway, mounting them there in rows.

The cards added comfort to the increasingly dilapidated house. Long retired from work, she had very little government assistance on which to live. The house was run-down, the floors were creaky, the wallpaper was peeling off in spots, and the porch was rotting away. The little old lady cried out to the Lord for provision and help, but at times she was forced to search neighborhood trash receptacles for food to eat.

One glad day, after many years, she received word from her son that he was returning home for a visit. On the day of his arrival she awoke early, prepared a delicious lunch for him, and dressed in her finest tattered clothes. She climbed into the old family car, which barely ran.

The happy old woman arrived at the pier just in time to see the ship dock. The gangway was lowered, and her son was one of the first passengers to come ashore. When their eyes met, he ran to his frail little mother, picked her up in his strong arms, and swung her around with a giant hug. Then he took a long, hard look at her.

"Mother, why are you wearing such tattered clothing . . . and why is the car running so roughly?" As they drove the short distance to her house, she explained without complaint, "Well, son, it hasn't been easy at times, but I've done just fine with what I have."

As they arrived, he took one look at the rotting porch and

said, "Why have you let the house go into such disrepair while I've been gone?"

Again she graciously replied, "Son, when you are elderly, you must sometimes learn to do without."

They stepped through the front door and into the long open hallway. When he saw the postcards she had stapled to the walls, he was incredulous. *"Mother, what have you done?"* he cried desperately.

She smiled and said, "Son, I have kept every one of your beautiful postcards to remember you by. I've shared them with all my friends and displayed them here for all to see. There were far too many for me to carry."

"Mother!" he wailed. "Those aren't postcards! Those are *money orders!*"

Friend, Jesus Christ has paid our debt and provided each of us with money orders, or, as Peter wrote, "all things that pertain unto life and godliness . . . exceeding great and precious promises" (2 Peter 1:3–4). Instead of cashing in those promises and standing firmly on them, many of us live like homeless, helpless, hopeless paupers.

It is time for us to break free of our former relationship with the enemy. Satan is lawless, rebellious, and will do anything he can to ruin our kingdom effectiveness and keep us from reaching our kingdom potential. We must deal ruthlessly with him, cut him off, and send him away! Jesus said in Matthew 11:12 (NIV), "The kingdom of heaven has been forcefully advancing, and forceful men lay hold of it."

Thirty years ago, after years of fighting with intimidating and accusing thoughts, I discovered how to disable and disarm the enemy—I learned how to cash God's money orders. The steps that I took freed me from satanic accusation and self-condemnation. We'll continue to lay the foundation for our freedom, and once we have completed it, we'll take those final liberating steps together. But for now, let's consider *excess baggage*.

CHAPTER FOUR

Excess Baggage

As I stood in line at the Air France ticket counter at Houston's George Bush International Airport, in full view of the two hundred people waiting in line behind her, an elegantly dressed African lady pulled a new computer monitor (not a flat screen) from its shipping container, opened up her two suitcases on the floor, and began digging for a place to cram her new monitor, stuffing clothes everywhere.

Why? Airlines have baggage limitations. They restrict the number of pieces each passenger can bring on board, as well as the weight and sizes of those items. Nonetheless, although she had one too many packages, there was no way this woman was not taking her new purchase with her to Africa.

Overloading a plane can affect its handling in flight, which could lead to disaster. Spiritually speaking, *excess baggage* in your life will deter the progress of your growth. Your extra spiritual baggage may be related to your past or to your predecessors (parents and grandparents). Are you as intent as this traveler was to be free of your excess baggage? Let's look at what that might entail.

EVIL TWINS: CULTS AND THE OCCULT

Many Christians have come to the Lord only after a long quest for spiritual knowledge; in their searches they delved into God-forbidden things. Others, in moments of weakness, even after becoming Christians, have drifted into occult practices. In His Word, God repeatedly reveals His anger against these elements, and in this context He proclaims that He is a jealous God.[1]

The occult is clearly more dangerous than other offenses because it involves the act of soliciting and securing supernatural power from sources other than God. The devil and his demons take very seriously the commitment a person makes to connect with them. Satan wants to protect any demonic ties to you, whether they were established years ago or last week.

Occult activities include Ouija,™ séances, Freemasonry, fortune-telling, Dungeons and Dragons,™ astrology, witchcraft, satanism, demonic video games, Pokemon,™ and *Harry Potter* books. (See Appendix B for a more comprehensive list and more instruction.) The word *witchcraft* comes from the Middle English *wicchecraft* (from *wicca,* "wizard"), which refers to practicing "sorcery," which is the meaning of the Greek word *pharmakeia;* this is the term from which has come the English word *pharmacy,* a place that prepares and dispenses drugs. Consequently, abusing drugs, legal or illegal, also opens the door to witchcraft spirits.

Along with the occult are cults and false religions, such as Mormonism, Islam, Hinduism, Scientology, Unitarianism, Buddhism, etc.[2]

A Plea for Perseverance

I wonder: how many readers have made it to this point in *Breaking the Enemy's Grip*? Experience tells me that only a fraction of those who purchase this book will actually read, absorb, and apply these truths. No matter what I write, how well it's written, or how many copies are sold, only a small percentage will follow through to completion. Why? I believe there are two basic reasons.

The first has to do with *motivation*. Three things generally motivate us: desperation, inspiration, and/or curiosity. Beyond curiosity, you're reading this book because you are either desperate or inspired, and that's wonderful—that's how the Holy Spirit draws us into change. You are either trying to find a remedy to what you perceive as a painful situation or you are striving to reach a goal that excites and compels you.

The second reason is that for every new revelation you receive, every page you turn, and every new commitment you make to Christ, *Satan is losing his grip on your life*. So I am focused now on the hungry soul who has continued reading to this point. With perseverance like yours, you can realize your true freedom in Christ and reach your ultimate kingdom potential! Satan will tempt you to give up, to surrender to him or to your flesh. Should that fail, he will try to distract you with other people or priorities. If you have a high degree of integrity, he'll remind you of your other obligations. Simply put, Satan cannot afford to allow you to finish this book and this process—he has too much at stake.

Please allow me to stop here and pray for you:

Father, in the name of your Son and my Savior, Jesus Christ, right now I am asking you to surround the one who is reading these words with your holy angels. I am asking you, Holy Spirit, to maintain the momentum that brought my reader this far on the journey. Whether it's frustration with life as it is, or inspiration to be the person he or she can and should become, please work in his or her heart until each receives true freedom from the enemy's clutches and reaches the highest level of kingdom potential in Christ. Amen.

Why should you press on? In the preface of our book *Spiritual Housecleaning,* we raise the following question.

Imagine there was a plague of snakes of biblical proportions in your city. The house in which you live is completely overrun with deadly, poisonous snakes. How important would it be for you to make sure some of the snakes were removed? You wouldn't even consider that an option, would you? Absolutely not. You would insist that all of the snakes be removed if you and your family were to continue living there. Could you sleep peacefully if you thought there might be even one poisonous snake left in your home?

As we lay the foundation for our freedom, we will come face to face with some disconcerting things that, like venomous serpents, will have polluted our hearts and lives, if not our homes. I discovered how spiritually debilitating they were in my life. Since then, I've assisted literally thousands of Christians around the world in experiencing freedom from their excess baggage of ancestral bondage (or generational iniquity), mental torment, physical maladies, satanic attacks, and emotional pain.

ANCESTRAL INIQUITY

The first of these crippling issues, ancestral bondage (or generational iniquity), is something over which you have no control. In fact, like the color of your eyes, you were born with it. Perhaps you're asking, "Why should I be concerned about sins that someone else committed? Especially someone who may have lived one hundred and fifty years ago?"

It's simple, really. When people sin, they open the door to the demonic realm. (For example, see Ephesians 4:26-27.) Depending on the nature of their sin and degree to which they submitted themselves to it, they can easily enter into partnership with the devil. As they yield themselves to him, their actions serve him rather than God. (See Romans 6:12-16.)[3] Satan then takes advantage of unholy bonds that, left untouched, move from one generation to the next. These impure soul ties are spiritual alliances or contracts that have been established through the sins of our forefathers—you might visualize this as a spiritual umbilical cord connecting generations. Exodus 34:7 says,

[The LORD God is] keeping mercy for thousands, forgiving iniquity and transgression and sin, and that will by no means clear the guilty; visiting the iniquity of the fathers upon the children, and upon the children's children, unto the third and to the fourth generation.

Notice it speaks of the father's "iniquity." The word *iniquity* carries the thought of "being bent."; a *bent* is an inclination or tendency that, when acted upon, can result in overt wickedness. We sometimes talk about someone with "a bent to do something"; for example, the drug-addicted son of an alcoholic father was "born with a bent toward addiction." A familiar quotation is "as the twig is bent, so grows the tree." Each of us was born with facial features, hair, eyes, and skin color resulting from our parents. Our parents can also impart to us our personality traits, strengths and weaknesses, and even our susceptibility to certain illnesses.

Intentional and habitual sin can become a legally binding spiritual contract (or agreement) that one knowingly or unknowingly makes with the enemy. The consequences of our forefathers' iniquity may be our tendencies toward certain sins (e.g., lying, stealing, phobias, perversion, alcoholism, fear, anger, rage, etc.); sicknesses and diseases (e.g., heart trouble, high blood pressure, cancer, mental illness, depression, etc.); even spiritual and emotional weakness. It can also involve demonic bondage in terms of familiar spirits (evil spirits that operate within families and who can appear in ghostlike forms posing as spirits of the departed).

When a person is involved with a cult or the occult—or, for that matter, ungodliness of any sort—he or she opens doors and can become contractually bound to evil spirits who operate in darkness. We know from the horrors of slavery that a slave gives birth to a slave. In the case of generational iniquity children and grandchildren will be born not with the guilt of their parents' sins, but with a proclivity toward the same failures. And often their progeny knowingly or unknowingly "renew the lease" with Satan by their own similar sin, extending the iniquity beyond four generations.

When Nehemiah learned that the exiles rebuilding Jerusalem had found the city in ruins, he went directly to the Lord:

> *When I heard this, I sat down and wept. I mourned for days, fasting and praying before the God-of-Heaven.*
>
> *I said, "GOD, God-of-Heaven, the great and awesome God, loyal to his covenant and faithful to those who love him and obey his commands: Look at me, listen to me. Pay attention to this prayer of your servant that I'm praying day and night in intercession for your servants, the People of Israel, confessing the sins of the People of Israel. And I'm including myself, I and my ancestors, among those who have sinned against you"* (Nehemiah 1:4–6 THE MESSAGE).

One Important Clarification

It *is* absolutely true that when Jesus said "It is finished" as He died for our sins, His work *was* finished—all of it. In His death God laid on Him "the iniquity of us all" (Isaiah 53:6), and thus all our iniquity was paid for. Some therefore argue that Jesus' death cancelled all ancestral curses, but Paul says that Jesus came to redeem us specifically *from the curse of the law* (Galatians 3:13). Consequences of our sin can still remain, as Jesus revealed in a case that *didn't* involve ancestral sin.[4]

Please note: Scripture is completely clear that *we are not guilty of our parents' sins or iniquities.* We are each responsible and accountable for ourselves—our *own* sins and iniquity, as Ezekiel said:

> The parent will die for what the parent did, for the sins of oppressing the weak, robbing brothers and sisters, doing what is dead wrong in the community.
>
> Do you need to ask, "So why does the child not share the guilt of the parent?" Isn't it plain? It's because the child did what is fair and right. Since the child was careful to do what is lawful and right, the child will live truly and well.
>
> The soul that sins is the soul that dies. The child does not share the guilt of the parent, nor the parent the guilt of the child. If you live upright and well, you get the credit; if you live a wicked life, you're guilty as charged. (Ezekiel 18:18-20 THE MESSAGE)

You might ask, "If I'm not guilty of the iniquities of my fathers, and Christ has fully paid for them, then why must I bother with my fathers' iniquity?" The answer is that you may not be living out the truth about yourself, confronting and countering the lies of the accuser. If you do not live in light of the truth and impose that truth upon the enemy, he will continue to harass you with lies.

If you are carrying the excess baggage of ancestral iniquity, it is *imperative* that you cast it off. Once you begin to take the steps to freedom that I've outlined in the last chapter, you will be instructed to make a list of sins and iniquity in which your parents or grandparents participated. Some family sins are obvious; however, you should ask the Holy Spirit to show you anything He specifically wants you to renounce. The purpose is neither to cast blame on past generations nor to make an all-inclusive list; the point is to list those things that God finds significant to your freedom. (And remember: We are to confess our *sins,* not our temptations or inclinations to sin.) Let's continue identifying excess baggage.

TRAUMA

Sarah was the cutest little two-year-old you've ever seen. She was crowned with curly blond hair that glistened in the sunlight, and she had big beautiful blue eyes that twinkled when she smiled. And Sarah smiled a lot. Hers was a happy family.

One morning, several hours after her father had left for work, a fire started in the heating system of the apartment complex in which Sarah's family lived. Her mother had stepped outside to hang her wet laundry, when suddenly she saw smoke drifting from the neighboring windows. Seconds later flames were engulfing her apartment, and instantly she realized what was happening. Running back toward the open door, she screamed, "Fire! Somebody, help! My baby . . . my baby!" But as she tried to reenter to reach little Sarah, billows of thick black smoke drove her back. She coughed and gagged as masked firemen with breathing apparatus ran past her into the burning apartment.

In mere moments, which seemed like an eternity to Sarah's mother, a brave young fireman emerged from the smoldering building with baby Sarah dangling from his arms.

One rescuer cried, "She's not breathing! We don't know if we'll be able to save her or not!" They laid Sarah on the ground and frantically began to give her mouth-to-mouth resuscitation. Her seemingly lifeless body soon began to respond as she gasped and began to breathe, color returning to her little cheeks.

All of the above was what could be seen. But there is an unseen realm that is coexistent with the physical world in which we live. The spirit world is not only real, it is primary—it preceded the physical world. Before anything was made, there was God, who is spirit. As mysterious as it seems to our earthbound minds, the spirit world is *the substance,* and the physical world is only *the shadow.*

Sarah was traumatized by the screams of her mother, the smell of the smoke, and the onrush of masked firemen. Her soul—comprised of her mind, will, and emotions—was in shock. In abject fear, she cried for help, and lingering demonic spirits swept in to "comfort her."

Why would demonic spirits want to comfort her? Evil spirits will be whatever they need to be in order to get what they want or to keep what they have. And what they want most is a physical body to inhabit. Just as Sarah's mother had left the apartment door open when she stepped outside to hang the laundry, in Sarah's trauma the door of her soul was thrown open wide to demonic spirits that took advantage of her. Internationally known author and speaker George Otis Jr. says, "In trauma, the soul solicits many saviors." Yet one day these "spirit friends" will turn on her. Her "saviors" will become her masters.[5]

(It is fair to ask the question, "Why doesn't this happen to everyone who experiences a trauma?" Maybe because of their personalities—people have different levels of susceptibility. Or perhaps because some are being protected by the prayers of loved ones. Or even simply because demons cannot be every-where at all times. But it is true that trauma doesn't always result in spiritual transactions.)

As a teenager, things began to go sour for Sarah. She intentionally began making wrong choices and forming alli-ances with the wrong crowd. The spirits that had attached themselves to her in her childhood trauma, at this point, because of her sinful choices, were given the opportunity to attract other evil spirits like themselves and thus build a stronghold with which to keep her in bondage. Demonic attachments in a person's life can be the result of generational iniquity (passed on to them at birth from their parents); the result of personal sin (choices); or the result of traumatic experiences (like Sarah's). Let's look at some other examples.

When a three-year-old boy's father deserts his mother, or dies unexpectedly, the young boy has no capacity to ade-quately process the matter and deal with his pain. He simply goes to sleep one night in a two-parent home and awakes the next day fatherless. He can understand neither death nor the intricacies of a marriage relationship. Thus, he is likely to conclude that his daddy left because he (the child) was a bad boy. After all, he reasons, had he been a good boy, his daddy would never have left the family.

As he grows older, he concludes that the boys at school who have dads are the good boys. They deserve fathers. A mental stronghold is built that says, *I don't deserve a daddy*. This is one way the devil and his minions take advantage of child-hood trauma.

How does a beaten or molested child becomes demon-ized? The soul is the gatekeeper of life. In a traumatic expe-rience, your mind, will, and emotions can become compro-mised (traumatized), because the gates of your life have been thrown open. In some cases, though not every case, the enemy uses that moment to sweep in like a flood and attach himself, utilizing that opening to get a toehold in your life. A toehold can become a foothold that ultimately becomes a stronghold.

The devil is in no hurry; he will often wait until the victim reaches adulthood to release evil spirits that begin to steal, kill, and destroy.[6] It is here that addictions set in and uncontrollable temper takes hold. Years after the trauma, the enemy emerges to express himself openly and freely.

It's easy for most of us to understand how the Holy Spirit comes to live in us as a result of our response to the gospel. We know that His goal is to manifest His holy life through our mortal bodies. Therefore, we should also be able to understand how unholy spirits attach themselves to our lives as a result of our response to them; we should know that their goal is to someday manifest their unholy lives through our mortal bodies. It may be mysterious, but it's no mystery.

One night we were ministering at the altar of our church, when Margaret, a Christian woman with whom the senior pastor was praying, began to manifest a demonic presence. The pastor called me over to assist him.

I said to the spirit, "What is your name?"

The spirit in the woman answered in a gruff, unearthly voice, "Burn."

"Burn is your name?" I asked, to be certain. The spirit said yes. I thought to myself, *Burn is a strange name.*

So I stopped the process and asked, "Margaret, were you ever involved in a fire?"

She told us a story much like Sarah's. She was trapped in a burning house when she was only eighteen months old. The entire family thought she was surely dead.

As we began to minister again, I spoke firmly to the demonic spirit, who looked up at me. "Burn! You leave her now in the name of Jesus." Quickly the spirit calling itself Burn, which had been attached to Margaret for more than forty years, departed. At last she was at peace. Then she gratefully explained that her aged mother had often said she hoped to see her daughter set free before she died. That week Margaret was able to report to her mother, "Your prayers for me have been answered. I'm free!" Within a few months her mother went to be with the Lord, and for several years Margaret continued to remind and assure me that something was broken off from her that night, allowing her to experience God as never before.

CHRISTIAN VICTIMIZATION

One night at a backyard prayer meeting, a young Ohio housewife tearfully confessed to Alice: "When I saw you and your husband holding your new baby boy, my heart was filled with envy. Your life seemed so perfect. Until recently I too was pregnant, but I miscarried my baby. Please forgive me for my envy and for hating you because you have a beautiful healthy baby and I have none."

We acutely understood the woman's feelings. Alice explained to her that only one year earlier, she had also miscarried our first child during her pregnancy. Unfortunately, many Christians put people with public ministries on pedestals. They fantasize what it must be like to have the "perfect marriage" or "ideal family." Perhaps it's the influence of Hollywood and Madison Avenue, or maybe it's simply human imagination run wild. Deep inside, we insist on resolution, and we thrive on fairytale stories with happy endings. With today's clever publicity spins, we often don't know fact from fiction. Even if we did, rather than accepting life as it truly is (with the good, the bad, and the ugly), we are intent on mentally reconstructing things to please ourselves.

During the past fifty years, I have witnessed in the

Western church the gradual development of a "Christian victimization" culture. Prior to that, believers largely considered life's ups and downs a reality to be expected while living on a sin-cursed planet. They understood that God even uses trouble as a tool to fashion us into the image of His Son. Have we forgotten Jesus' words?

> *"If the people of this world hate you, just remember that they hated me first. . . . Remember how I told you that servants are not greater than their master. So if people mistreat me, they will mistreat you. If they do what I say, they will do what you say. They will do it because you belong to me, and they don't know the one who sent me. . . . While you are in the world, you will have to suffer. . . . But cheer up! I have defeated the world"* (John 15:18, 20–21; 16:33 CEV).

Or the admonition of James, Jesus' brother?

> *My friends, be glad, even if you have a lot of trouble.*
> (James 1:2 CEV)

What's happened to us? The Western church has embraced pop-psychology's implication that lack of self-love, low self-esteem, difficulty paying attention, or any feelings of rejection are abnormal, and they promise that everyone's life can be easily adjusted with enough counseling and medication. (When I was a child, ADHD (attention deficit/hyperactivity disorder) was called *boyhood!*)

Unfortunately, many Christians in recent years have also embraced an unbiblical health-and-wealth theology built around the supremacy of human needs over divine purposes. Spewing from many of America's pulpits is the concept of a God in *our* image who exists to meet *our* needs and who, when necessary, will set aside His purposes on a moment's notice to see that we are pain- and problem-free.

Award-winning actor Johnny Depp, recently interviewed on a U.S. television talk show, was asked what has changed the most during his fifteen years of acting. Without hesitation he replied, "When I began my movie career, it was standard to see the lead actor display flaws in his character; even his physical features were imperfect. But today the moviegoer wants to see leading men who are perfect in every way. This bothers me because none of us live in a perfect world."[7]

Add to this Hollywood's images of a perfect love story, an ideal marriage, and a they-lived-happily-ever-after ending, and we're left with a culture of victimization. The twisted teachings of self-obsession and prosperity theology have debilitated the American church and have been destructive to the spread of the true gospel of Christ.

In my travels to Africa, India, and other places, I have discovered Christians who believe the Bible without question. They are convinced that suffering is a normal and necessary part of their to-be-expected experience, that it's actually built into God's plan. They understand that through our suffering God glorifies himself in us, teaches us total dependence upon Him, enlarges our capacity to trust Him alone, and humiliates the devil. These faith-filled believers know they're more than Satan's conquerors in Christ, and they're convinced that no one becomes an overcomer until something has truly been overcome. One young Indian minister recently told me, "It would be my greatest joy to suffer for Christ's sake."

God intended that the church walk in spiritual dominion, not be spiritually dominated. Yet the demonic world is working overtime to victimize Western Christians. Because of their anxiety, even many believers are now drug-dependent, living as those without hope, convinced that God has failed them.

They have believed the lie that to be saved is to be sanitized from suffering.

Once again, it is tragic but true that many who are the bride of Christ are living as outcasts when they should be reigning and ruling. They are living as servants, or worse, as strangers.[8] Victimized believers watch their favorite Christian television personalities and read the books of their favorite Christian authors and then fantasize what it must be like to live such "charmed lives." They typically have no idea what severe life-challenges and tragedies those that they idolize have endured. Believe it: What doesn't kill you makes you strong.

Worry is the sin of calling into question the integrity of God. When we embrace the spirit of victimization through self-pity, we open ourselves to demonic influences, just as would be the case if we embraced any other sin. From that point, our minds are playgrounds in which evil spirits can romp.

Later, when we go through the steps to freedom, you will be given an opportunity to deal decisively with the excess baggage of the occult, ancestral iniquity, trauma, and victimization. Until you stop toting those bags, you'll never be able to live as Christ intends for you to live.

I take absolutely no pride in the fact that my great-great-grandfather was a southern slave owner. I am grateful, however, that even though he was ignorant about the evils of slavery, he was known throughout the county as a benevolent man, so much so that when the slaves were emancipated in 1863, a strange thing happened. Several of his elderly slaves sent a representative to tell him, "Mastuh Smith. We knows we been freed. But you been a good mastuh. We don't know nothin' but slavin'. Bein' free means startin' all ovuh. So, I'z been sent to ask, 'Can we keep on slavin' for you till we die?'"

Sadly, this is also the lament of some Christians. They have been freed from sin, but slaving is all they know. They continue to yield to temptation and allow themselves to be conformed to the world, instead of being transformed by the renewing of their minds.[9] I encourage you today to choose freedom!

CHAPTER FIVE

The Call to Forgive

One day Simon Peter asked Jesus, "How many times must I forgive someone who offends me? Is seven times enough?" No doubt Peter had heard in the synagogue that, according to rabbinical law, one was to forgive up to three times. Peter's offer to forgive someone *seven* times certainly seemed more than generous from his perspective.

Jesus essentially replied, "Not seven times, Peter, but seventy times seven. Stop counting." Then He told His disciples this story.

Once upon a time, there was a king who decided to collect all of his debts. He brought in his debtors and demanded that they pay their bills.

One man who owed fifty million silver coins explained that he was unable to pay. The king immediately ordered that he, his wife and children, and all that he owned should be sold to repay the debt.

The man dropped to his knees and begged, "Have mercy, my Lord. Somehow, someday, I promise I will pay every cent I owe!"

The king, touched by the man's plea, relented and graciously cancelled the entire debt, freeing him and his family.

When the newly forgiven man left the palace, he happened upon a man who owed him a small debt of one hundred *silver coins. Mercilessly he grabbed his debtor by the throat and demanded, "Pay me everything you owe me, NOW!"*

The other man also dropped to his knees, begging, "Please, sir, give me some time, and I promise to repay you." But the first man insisted that his debtor be immediately thrown into jail until he paid all he owed.

Some bystanders who witnessed his harsh treatment reported it, and the king had him arrested and brought before the throne. "You are an evil man," the king said. "When you begged me for mercy, I cancelled your debt entirely and set you free. Shouldn't you have shown the same mercy to others?"

The king was so angry that he ordered the man to be released to the tormentors *until he had repaid every cent.* *"That,"* Jesus said, *"is exactly how my heavenly Father will treat you, if you refuse to forgive those who offend you"* (Matthew 18:21–35, paraphrased).

WHY FORGIVE?

We Are to Forgive Because God Commands It

There is no clearer expression of God's command to forgive than in Colossians 3:13, where Paul writes, "Be eventempered, content with second place, quick to forgive an offense. Forgive as quickly and completely as the Master forgave you" (THE MESSAGE). If for no other reason, we should forgive others because God demands it.

And we are to forgive unilaterally—we are not to wait for

an apology. With the possible exception of the thief on the cross,[1] there is no biblical record of anyone ever asking Jesus for forgiveness. Regardless, just as he did with the adulterous woman who was about to be stoned,[2] Jesus continually forgave sinners, always taking the initiative. Even in dying, He prayed, "Father, forgive them, for they do not know what they are doing."[3] Why forgive? Because Jesus came to earth to reconcile us to himself; now we are the ministers of reconciliation.[4]

We Are to Forgive Because God Has Forgiven Us

In the story Jesus told, the man whose massive debt had been forgiven refused to forgive his own debtor of a relatively small obligation. It was the height of ingratitude for him not to pass along the forgiveness he had received.

My dad, Robert E. Smith, a faithful preacher for more than fifty years, taught me that *everything God gives me was on its way to someone else when I received it. My assignment is to make sure that it reaches them.*

God has showered us with love so that we can love others. He has lavished grace upon us in order that we may be gracious. He has forgiven us of our offenses against Him to enable us to forgive those who will offend us.

My dad asked me one day, "Son, why does God forgive your sins?" I knew he wasn't looking for an obvious answer, so I admitted that I didn't know. He said, "Look at Psalm 51 for your answer." I turned to it and read, "Create in me a clean heart, O God; and renew a right spirit within me. . . . *Then will I teach transgressors thy ways; and sinners shall be converted unto thee*" (emphasis added). Even when cleansing us, God's heart is set toward evangelism!

We Are to Forgive Lest We Destroy Ourselves

Unforgiveness is unhealthy; in fact, it's a killer. Our minds are intricately linked to our bodies. Negative emotions result in chemical reactions that will, over time, trigger sickness and disease. Proverbs 14:30 (NIV) says, "A heart at peace gives life to the body, but envy rots the bones." Unforgiveness does more damage to the vessel in which it's stored than to the person on which it's poured!

When someone lives to be 100, the rest of us wonder how he or she did it. What's the secret? When the late great entertainer Bob Hope was asked how he lived to be 100 years old, he said his first rule was not to bicker with others:

> *"I am not one to widen any quarrel. I actually talk to myself about not getting uptight. I psyche myself. I don't need silly arguments. It will only hurt me if I'm negative. I don't even want to refuse to give an autograph because it's bad for me. . . . I try never to get too racked up about anything."*[5]

Hating your ex-spouse, for example, will not likely hurt him or her, but it will eventually destroy *you*. It will rot you from the inside out. You will find your spirit becoming deadened toward the Lord. Then your mind, will, and emotions will be increasingly hardened. Bitterness will fill your mind and heart. Eventually you will hate yourself because you're so hateful. Paranoia will overtake you, and you'll begin feeling that everyone is out to get you.

Churches are filled with overmedicated Christians, many of whom have no medical problem at all. They are filled with bitterness, resentment, hatred, and unforgiveness toward others. America's mental hospitals are filled with people who've lost their minds for the same reason. Unforgiveness, like a cancer, will ultimately attack and destroy your health.

We Are to Forgive to Avoid Being Tormented

Twenty-three-year-old Susan came to us for counseling. She hadn't spoken to her parents since she was seventeen; her father had sexually molested her when she was a tiny girl. Although he had confessed his offense and asked for her forgiveness, memories of his sin haunted her day and night, driving her to loose living, drunkenness, and addiction to prescription drugs.

When we met Susan, she was being treated for depression in a psychiatric hospital in Houston. After two weeks of counseling and therapy, with few results, Susan's doctor referred her to our church for ministry. When she arrived by taxi, she was taken to a room where a team of loving, godly women ministered to her in prayer.

They had several deliverance sessions with Susan; I sat in on one of her last ones. "Susan," I said. "What your father did to you as a child was terrible. A man who would do such a thing to his daughter is without excuse!" As I said this, every muscle in her body tightened in anger and resentment.

I went on. "In fact, Susan, a man like your father, who would do to a little girl what he did to you, should be humiliated." This also rang true in her heart—for years she'd been feeling it. *How can he get away with this?* she'd thought. *Everyone thinks he's an honorable man. I cannot allow him to escape paying the penalty for his sin. He must pay for what he's done.*

Susan had not been able to forgive her father. Contrary to what most of us would think, her inability to forgive him wasn't because she was bad but because she was created in God's image. It is God who said in Ezekiel 18:20, "The soul that sinneth, it shall die," and in Romans 3:23, "The wages of sin is death."

Perhaps you too have been harboring unforgiveness toward someone who has betrayed you. Deep inside, you reason that it would be unjust to release him without seeing him pay for his sin. You feel compelled to see that justice is served. You are demanding justice, a payment for sin . . . just as God does. Just like you, God hates sin. But here's the issue: Jesus already took the punishment, made the payment, and forever satisfied justice. When you refuse to forgive, you are denying that the blood of Christ covers that specific offense.

Like Susan, many believers are being unnecessarily tormented, mentally, emotionally, and/or physically. It could be a result of tormenting relationships, tormenting thoughts, tormenting circumstances, or tormenting health. Why are they being tormented? Because they are harboring unforgiveness in their hearts.

Jesus taught that when we refuse to forgive others for something they have done to us, *we prevent God from forgiving us:* "In prayer there is a connection between what God does and what you do. You can't get forgiveness from God, for instance, without also forgiving others. If you refuse to do your part, you cut yourself off from God's part" (Matthew 6:14–15 THE MESSAGE). In the Lord's Prayer, Christ even taught us to pray, "Keep us forgiven with you and forgiving others" (Matthew 6:12 THE MESSAGE).

Worse still, Jesus teaches that when we refuse to forgive others, God will release us to "the tormentors." Notice the conviction in the parable:

> *O thou wicked servant, I forgave thee all that debt, because thou desiredst me: Shouldest not thou also have had compassion on thy fellow servant, even as I had pity on thee? And his lord was wroth, and delivered him to the tormentors, till he should pay all that was due unto him.* (Matthew 18:32–34)

The church has largely ignored these closing words: "So likewise shall my heavenly Father do also unto you, if ye from your hearts forgive not every one his brother their trespasses" (Matthew 18:35). Whoa! This is serious. If we refuse the sacrifice of Jesus' blood as payment for someone's offense against us, God will deliver us to the tormentors. What does that mean, exactly? I'm not sure, but believe me, you don't want it.

Susan was sobbing uncontrollably as I continued. "Susan, a man who would do what your father did to you should be arrested." Her teeth clenched as her hands gripped the arms of her chair. "He should be beaten." She began rocking back and forth, nodding in agreement. "Susan, a man like him should be *crucified*!"

Suddenly God's revelation melted the place in her heart where she'd stored up vengeance. Instantly she realized that she no longer needed to hold her father hostage to her emotions. She no longer needed to ensure that her father paid for his sins—*Jesus already had*. (Jesus not only paid the price for *our* sins on Calvary, He also paid the price for every offense that has ever been or ever will be committed *against* us.)

This piercing revelation punctured the balloon of Susan's bitterness. She wept and repented for refusing to forgive her father. As though he were in the room with us, she said, "Daddy, I forgive you . . . I forgive you. I'm so sorry."

Then an astonishing thing occurred: Susan began to experience spontaneous deliverance. The team and I watched in amazement as she coughed and gagged, a seemingly endless parade of evil spirits leaving her. When I asked, "Lord, what's happening?" I felt Him say, *I'm removing the tormenters—they are no longer necessary*. Within moments, a complete peace settled over her.

That was more than fifteen years ago. Just recently I received a beautiful letter from Susan, including a picture of her happy family and her testimony of God's wonderful deliverance. She is now a strong intercessory prayer leader in her church. *To God be the glory!*

If there is anyone—living or dead—against whom you are

harboring unforgiveness, resentment, hatred, or the like, I can emphatically say that *you are already being tormented*. I can also assure you that it will get worse, not better, as time goes on.

Does Jesus want to release us to the tormentors? Absolutely not. But when we refuse to forgive those who have hurt, offended, or betrayed us, we choose to be their judge and jury. At that point we are sitting in judgment, a position reserved for God himself. When we arrogantly attempt to replace Him, He has no other option than to release us to demonic tormentors for discipline until we learn to repent and to forgive even as we have been forgiven.

Friend, I've seen prayer warriors fervently and passionately intercede for a person who was harboring unforgiveness against another, even rebuking the tormenters. But the person for whom they are praying will never be free from torment until he or she personally releases and forgives the one who caused the offense. Why? Because, as Jesus taught, God has allowed torment in response to their refusal to forgive as He commands.

We Are to Forgive Because Unforgiveness Grieves the Holy Spirit

We know that the Bible warns us not to grieve the Holy Spirit. But have you noticed the context in which that warning appears? How does one actually grieve Him, and what is it that breaks His heart?

> *Don't make God's Spirit sad. [Grieve not the Holy Spirit.] The Spirit makes you sure that someday you will be free from your sins. Stop being bitter and angry and mad at others. Don't yell at one another or curse each other or ever be rude.* Instead, be kind and merciful, and forgive others, just as God forgave you because of Christ. *Do as God does. After all, you are his dear children. Let love be your*

guide. Christ loved us and offered his life for us as a sacrifice that pleases God. (Ephesians 4:30–5:2 CEV, emphasis added)

The Holy Spirit is grieved by our refusal to forgive others. Forgiveness requires God's power; forgiveness is a *God thing*. Forgiving is holy, compassionate, and kind; it expresses humility, patience, gentleness, and faith. Refusing to forgive is unholy, critical, and unkind; it expresses pride, impatience, anger, and unbelief. Paul and Silas refused to hate those who accused, arrested, and imprisoned them in the Philippian jail, choosing instead to trust God with their circumstance and praise Him in the midst of it, and a citywide revival resulted.

We Are to Forgive Because Unforgiveness Prevents God From Hearing and Answering Prayer

The psalmist wrote, "If I regard iniquity in my heart, the Lord will not hear me" (66:18). I love *The Message* rendering of this verse: "If I had been cozy with evil, the Lord would never have listened."

To regard sin is to disregard God. Please read carefully the following verses from the *Contemporary English Version*:

> *Someday you will beg the* LORD *to help you, but he will turn away because of your sins.* (Micah 3:4)

> *If my thoughts had been sinful, he would have refused to hear me. But God did listen and answered my prayer. Let's praise God! He listened when I prayed.* (Psalm 66:18–20)

> *Whenever you stand up to pray, you must forgive what others have done to you. Then your Father in heaven will forgive your sins.* (Mark 11:25–26)

> *If you are about to place your gift on the altar and remem-*

ber that someone is angry with you, leave your gift there in front of the altar. Make peace with that person, then come back and offer your gift to God. (Matthew 5:23–24)

OFFENSES OFFER US AN OPPORTUNITY

Count on it: Offenses *will* come your way. They are a natural result of living on this sin-cursed planet. Fallen men and women, in the strength of their flesh, *will* rise up on their own and strike you. Some offenses *will* cause you physical pain and discomfort. Others *will* cause you emotional hurt and embarrassment. Some people *will* unknowingly offend you without any evil intent whatsoever.

Since offenses are inevitable, here's the real issue: How will you respond to mistreatment? Will you elevate what you feel are your *rights* above your *responsibilities*? Will you elevate your need for *comfort* above your need to be *conformed* to Christ's image? Will you allow your experiences to define you, or will you allow the Lord to mold you? Offenses against us are like heavenly sandpaper God uses to shape us into the image of Jesus.

Though in this life we should expect tribulation, Jesus reminds us to be cheerful: "In this godless world you will continue to experience difficulties. But take heart! I've conquered the world" (John 16:33 THE MESSAGE). Why? Because "in all these things we are more than conquerors" (Romans 8:37). This verse in the *The Message* says, "None of this fazes us because Jesus loves us."

Offenses provide us with opportunities to prove the realities of our faith. They test our spiritual mettle. They show what we're made of. They force us to demonstrate our convictions, to put our spiritual money where our mouth is. Don't just say, "Jesus Christ is Lord"; He's looking for those who live it in their everyday lives when the heat is on.

UNFORGIVENESS IS UNNECESSARY

Resentment is a common result of being offended, so let's take a closer look at the word *resent*. The prefix *re* means "again." The suffix *sent* is from the Latin *sentir,* which means "to feel." When we *resent* someone, we are reserving the right to *re-feel* our anger against him or her.

Unforgiveness is claiming the right to punish someone who has offended us, harboring in our hearts the right to "get even." In contrast, to honor Christ, we must show mercy to those who have shown us no mercy. We must relinquish the prerogative to hurt those who have hurt us.

> *Our Scriptures tell us that if you see your enemy hungry,*
> *go buy that person lunch, or if he's thirsty, get him a drink.*
> *Your generosity will surprise him with goodness. Don't let evil*
> *get the best of you; get the best of evil by doing good.*
> (Romans 12:20–21 THE MESSAGE)

Unforgiveness is unnecessary because Christ has paid the price for all sin. He died for the sins of the world. No other sacrifice is needed.

HOW GOD DEALS WITH OUR UNFORGIVENESS

When we refuse to forgive, God deals with us on four levels.

- *Conviction.* Initially, God convicts us. Guilt is a powerful motivation for us to confess, repent, and return to Christ.[6] If we fail to respond to His conviction, He will chasten us.
- *Chastening.* When chastening us, God uses circumstances to get our attention. This could include sudden unemployment, financial difficulty, unexpected expenses, or many other factors. Hebrews 12:8 (CEV) says, "God cor-

rects all of his children, and if he doesn't correct you, then you don't really belong to him."

- *Scourging.* When the Lord is forced to scourge us, we're in serious trouble. Scourging is what Jesus referred to in His story of the king and the debtor; scourging is when God releases us to the tormentors. For instance, Paul warned the Corinthian believers about taking the Lord's Supper (Communion) with sin in their hearts: "Examine your motives, test your heart, come to this meal in holy awe. If you give no thought (or worse, don't care) about the broken body of the Master when you eat and drink, you're running the risk of serious consequences. That's why so many of you even now are listless and sick, and others have gone to an early grave" (1 Corinthians 11:28–30 THE MESSAGE).

- *The Sin Unto Death.* If we overlook God's conviction, chastening, and scourging, we literally run the risk of committing the sin unto death. This is the last thing the Lord wants to do, but if we proudly and arrogantly insist and persist, We leave Him no choice.[7] Let me tell you a sad story.

Jim was pastor of a large church in the northeast. Ray was a godly evangelist who was a faithful member of Jim's church and had been Jim's friend for more than two decades. Ray was an anointed man of impeccable character who loyally supported his pastor.

Due to no fault of Ray's, however, some people in the church were more attracted to his itinerant evangelistic ministry than they were to their own shepherd. Pastor Jim began to resent Ray and the favor God gave him with the people. Envy got its ugly grip on Jim's heart, and he began to speak evil of Ray—even from the pulpit.

One day I was asked by a church member to speak to

Pastor Jim regarding his relationship with Ray. I called the church and said, "Pastor Jim, this is Eddie Smith." After some small talk, I asked, "Jim, tell me something. Do you love Brother Ray?"

There was a long pause, and then he replied, "I don't have anything against the man."

I pressed further. "That's not what I asked you, Jim. I asked you if you love him."

He stammered for a moment and, gathering his courage, spat, "I don't think it's any of your business what I feel about him!" Then he hung up on me. I was shocked at the level of venom in his voice.

Two weeks later Pastor Jim, in his mid-forties, apparently in the prime of health and at the peak of his ministry, dropped dead of a heart attack.

I will always believe that Pastor Jim committed the sin unto death. You see, the Lord had sent others to speak to him as well, but he would neither listen nor repent. If we ignore God's conviction, chastening, and scourging, He may have no choice but to call us home. We who accept the responsibility of leadership carry a greater burden of accountability.[8]

But this isn't an issue only for ministers. *Each one of us* is a witness for Christ in this courtroom called Earth.

Our lost friends and relatives are the judge and jury, and Christ is on trial for a case of mistaken identity. The question they must answer is, "Who is He—Lord, or lunatic? Since he claimed to be God, he must be one or the other."

The Holy Spirit is the defense attorney pleading Christ's case, here to convince the lost world that Jesus *is* Lord. And again, we are His witnesses; we testify "in court," every day, for or against the defendant, Jesus.

All is well if we are good witnesses, but when our witness becomes clouded by sin, and our testimony isn't supporting the Holy Spirit's case, He will convict us so that we will repent and return to Him. If we do not, then He will chasten us. If we still refuse to repent, He will scourge us. And finally, if we do not turn back from our sin and become the witness Jesus needs in the courtroom, the Holy Spirit will take us on to heaven. Our witness must support the case—the eternal destiny of others is at stake.

GET OUT OF THE IMPORT/EXPORT BUSINESS

Some of the offenses we suffer are direct offenses aimed at us. Whether intentional or unintentional, they are committed against us individually and personally.

Others, however, are indirect offenses. These are sins that we've *imported* by picking up the offense of another. An example would be a wife who is angry with her husband's boss for the way he treats her husband. The offense isn't directed against her personally, but she has embraced her husband's offense as her own.

Even the good parts of our nature, our senses of justice and mercy, when misapplied, can cause us to react in ungodly ways. There is never a right way to do a wrong thing. Nevertheless, there are, in many cases, wrong ways to do the right thing. When we do them, we are wrong.

Sometimes we *export* our offenses by broadcasting them to others. We vent our hurt feelings, often in graphic detail, looking for comradeship. We think we're expressing our sense of justice, when, in fact, we're looking for someone to support us in our sin. Remember, our flesh is always reaching out for validation. When we refuse to forgive someone who has offended us, we're trying to validate hurt feelings, bitterness, resentment, and unforgiveness. Oddly, our search for validation eventually *in*validates us: We become *spiritual invalids*. We'd do well to get out of the import/export business.

IT'S A MATTER OF MISPLACED TRUST

When someone betrays you, you feel let down. Your trust has been violated. You received less than expected. As you consider what should or shouldn't have been done, your disappointment can easily turn to disdain. If you peel away the veneer, you will discover that the real problem was yours to begin with. Why? Because you were trusting the other person to be a certain way, and he or she didn't live up to your expectations.

Perhaps he or she wasn't even aware of your expectations. Regardless, the core issue is simple: You should have never imposed your expectations in the first place. You were wrong to hold up a standard (even if only in your own heart) for another person to meet. *You are to trust God, not people.*

Your tendency to trust man rather than God is so powerful that it is Scripture's center-point. That's right—the exact center of the Bible:

- The shortest chapter in the Bible is Psalm 117.
- The longest chapter in the Bible is Psalm 119.
- The center chapter of the Bible is Psalm 118. There are 594 chapters that precede and 594 chapters that follow Psalm 118.
- The total of 594 and 594 is 1,188.
- The center verse of the Bible is Psalm 118:8!

Here the psalmist writes, "It is better to trust in the LORD than to put confidence in man." As if to underscore His point, God says, in the next verse, "It is better to trust in the Lord than to put confidence in princes." He is jealous for our trust; we are to trust in Him with all our heart.[9]

THE FORK IN THE ROAD

Baseball legend Yogi Berra, known for his confusing use of the English language, once said, "When you come to a fork in the road . . . take it." Yogi didn't quite nail his point. But we can be certain that with every offense that comes our way, we *will* come to a fork in the road. One direction leads to freedom and life; the other leads to bondage and death. At that point you must always decide: Do you choose to forgive and love, or do you refuse to forgive and harbor unforgiveness?

We are promised in 1 Corinthians 10:13 (CEV): "You are tempted in the same way that everyone else is tempted. But God can be trusted not to let you be tempted too much, and he will show you how to escape from your temptations." There is no doubt we are individually responsible for forgiving those who offend us. When at that fork in the road— where one side leads to forgiveness and the other to unforgiveness—God will always show us the way of escape. When He does, as Yogi would say, "Take it!"

Now that we know *why* we should forgive, let's look at *how* we can forgive.

CHAPTER SIX

The Key to Forgiving

A Pennsylvania woman spent the better part of an hour shopping at a neighborhood grocery store without realizing that a passerby had stuck a knife into her neck, police said. . . .

Darlene Jones, 62, set out from home on foot before 7 A.M. [yesterday], when a running passerby slapped her on the back of the neck—or so she thought. She kept on going, as if nothing had happened.

Jones walked to the Acme supermarket in the nearby community of Yeadon, just outside Philadelphia, and bought a package of Oreo cookies and a newspaper before making the half-mile return journey to her house.

Only after she got home did her daughter notice the handle of a kitchen knife sticking out of her mother's neck. The daughter yanked out the blade, releasing a gush of blood, and quickly got her to the Hospital of the University of Pennsylvania, where she was listed in fair condition [today].

"Five or six people walked right past her without even

noticing," Darby Police Chief Robert Smythe told the Philadel-phia Inquirer, *while describing the incident as a "random, vicious attack."*

Supermarket surveillance cameras later showed the woman strolling through the aisles of the store, past clerks and custom-ers, with the knife handle clearly visible. Jones could not give police a description of her assailant, saying she did not even notice if it was a man or a woman.[1]

IDENTIFY THE WOUND

People who harbor unforgiveness are often quite certain of their target, acutely remembering both the offender and the nature of the offense. But for various reasons, just as Dar-lene Jones was oblivious to the blade in her neck, some of us ignore, overlook, minimize, and even deny our emotional wounds instead of confronting and resolving them. In *either* case, such pain frequently manifests in addictive behaviors such as compulsive drinking, illicit sex, drug abuse (including prescription drugs), pornography, and so on. Numbing our pain rather than dealing with it is foolish. If we expect to experience victory as overcomers in Christ, we must face our wounds and let the healing begin.

Sometimes, when counseling, I ask people if they're hold-ing any unforgiveness or bitterness in their hearts. Reflexively, they shake their heads no, assuming that I'll move on to another topic. Frequently, when I question further, I discover that in the recesses of their minds they have conveniently cov-ered their wounds with religious activity, hidden sin, busy-ness, humor, or any number of other things that shift the focus away from the real issues.

For instance, a person who was abused as a child may be a compulsive perfectionist. Whereas he had no control while being abused as a child, he now deals with emotional pain by exerting control over everything and everyone. He must have a perfect home, drive the perfect car, raise perfect children, and be married to the perfect spouse. He must attend the perfect church, which is of course led by the perfect pastor. Unchecked, his unrealistic expectations will ruin his relationships, especially within his family. He (or she) is likely to experience multiple marriages, hoping to find someone to trust while never learning how to love a spouse.

For example, my youngest brother, Tim Smith, is one tough hombre (as we say in Texas), a motorcycle policeman who eventually became chief of police. When we wrestled as children, he was no match for me; today, I'd be no match for him! Yet Tim has a serious weakness: He's allergic to bee and wasp stings. One sting, without proper first aid, and he could easily die.

However, some people don't die of a single wasp sting (metaphorically) but because of multiple, tiny ant bites. Their hearts are mortally wounded not by a single major incident but by many minor incidents through the years. Perhaps you can't remember specific past offenses that left you with festering resentment, rage, bitterness, or unforgiveness. You don't recall an isolated offense that wounded you spiritually, emotionally, verbally, or physically.

If you're in this category, it is the sum of multiple violations in your past that represents significant wounding in your heart. Rather than belaboring the point concerning whether (or to what degree) you've been wounded, ask God to reveal any unreconciled offenses that may be affecting you.

(Parenthetically, as a former pastor *and* the son of a pastor, I assure you that pastors and their families are well acquainted with these types of wounds. We are continual targets of both Satan and disgruntled church members. We're often expected to be thick-skinned, but the truth is we're just like everyone else. Pastors quickly learn that they can't please all of the people all of the time . . . and at times it seems we can hardly please anyone at all!)

Perhaps your offense came when you were a small child. You may not have known until now that you've been wrongly processing your feelings. That's not the point: Now that you do know the score, *from this moment on you are accountable.* Will you forgive and release your debtors so that today you can be forgiven and go free?

Regarding your offenders, perhaps you've been willing to *parole* (conditionally release) but are not yet willing to *pardon* (unconditionally release). Pardoning them means you unilaterally and completely release all your claims on them, just as God did for you. For some of us, that's a big deal!

CLEANSE THE WOUND

The healing begins as you cleanse the wound. (By *wound* I mean the offense you suffered at the hands of another.) To cleanse the wound, you must

(1) identify it;[2]
(2) repent of any sin you committed relating to it, including your failure to forgive;[3] and
(3) renounce the works of the enemy regarding it.[4]

We'll be doing this when we take our final steps to freedom (in chapter 10).

You might ask, "Aren't we to forgive and forget? I've been told that I haven't truly forgiven until I forget. How can I forget what was done to me?"

That's a great question, but *forgetting* isn't the focus; being released from your pain and bringing glory to God are the primary issues. A mother never forgets the pain of giving birth to her child, but in time her *memory* of the experience no longer hurts her. Similarly, you may always be able to recall the offense, but by taking proper care of the wound, in time your healing will be so complete and thorough that you'll be left with only a painless scar. The memory will no longer hurt. *True victory really isn't about forgetting—it's actually about your being able to remember the sins that were committed against you without feelings of resentment, and about your remembering your sins against God without feelings of guilt.*

When the first missionaries came to Labrador, they found no word for forgiveness in the Eskimo language, so they were forced to create one. Their word for forgiveness meant "not being able to think about it anymore." Even if you never forget the offense, when true forgiveness has occurred, two things will be true.

(1) You'll no longer have to think about the offense.
(2) If you do think about it, it will no longer cause you pain.

I rejoice to tell you that both of these are possible in Christ!

When I was in junior high, my parents went out of town and left my grandmother in charge. One day while they were gone, I came streaking down the hill in front of our home on my bicycle. With the wind in my hair I felt like motorcycle daredevil Evel Knievel; I didn't even notice the construction sand that had spilled onto our concrete driveway, so I didn't bother to apply the brakes as I made my usual sweeping turn. When my tires hit the sand, the concrete was instantly transformed into what seemed like a sheet of ice. The bicycle went one way, and I went the other. I made a perfect three-point landing . . . one of those points being my right elbow!

I ran into the house screaming at the top of my lungs, dripping blood everywhere. My matronly grandmother calmly walked me into the bathroom, opened the medicine cabinet, and found her preferred instrument of torture—a bright orange bottle of Merthiolate. She was going to cleanse my wound, and did she ever! She didn't even use the convenient little glass dauber; mercilessly she held my arm over the sink and poured that "liquid fire" all over my bloody elbow.

In my case, the greater pain of the treatment followed the pain of the accident. Nevertheless, in time, as adolescent boys tend to do, I sported my scar as a badge of honor. Today, more than fifty years later, the scar is still visible, the memory still accessible, but there is no pain at all associated with it. And yes, I have forgiven Grandma.

Confession, repentance, renunciation, and dissociation with darkness are like an antiseptic—they cleanse your wounded heart of the debris that would cause infection. Once the wound is *clean,* you are right to feel relieved, but the pain may still be easily recalled. So don't stop short: next, *close the wound.*

CLOSING THE WOUND

Jesus said, "I'm telling you to love your enemies. Let them bring out the best in you, not the worst" (Matthew 5:44 THE MESSAGE). Paul wrote in Romans 12:20, "If your enemies are hungry, give them something to eat. And if they are thirsty, give them something to drink" (CEV). In *The Message* it concludes with "Your generosity will surprise him with goodness." Acts of goodness toward those who have done us evil are the stitches that close the wound; each good deed you do for your offender actually adds a stitch to the wound that he left in your heart. Interestingly, Jesus never gives consideration to the severity of the offense; we must simply act as a matter of principle.

Michael, a thirty-something young professional, was right on time for his counseling appointment. Seated in my office, we began the small talk, and finally I said, "Michael, tell me about your relationship with your father."

He looked surprised. "I don't suppose I have a relationship with him."

"Oh, you definitely have a relationship with him," I replied. "The question is, *what kind* of relationship do you have?"

"Well, we haven't spoken in several years," he explained.

"Why?"

"Dad and I just don't get along."

At that, I pushed my telephone to his side of my desk, handed him my American Express card, and said, "Michael, I want you to call 1–800-FLOWERS."

"Why?"

"Today you're going to send a $50 bouquet of flowers to your dad."

"But he's an elderly man—he won't care anything about flowers."

"Michael," I said with a smile, "it's *my* credit card. Go ahead."

A moment later he mumbled, "The saleslady wants to know what to put on the card."

"Tell her to write: *Dad, I miss you. I've been thinking about you lately. Can we get together soon? Love, Michael.*"

After he'd hung up, with a shrug he asked, "What about my counseling?"

"You just received it," I said. "I'll see you next week."

He left my office more than a bit puzzled.

———

The next day Michael returned to my office, breathless and unannounced. "You'll never guess what happened," he gushed. "My mother called and said, 'Son, a floral delivery-man came to our house this morning. Your dad answered the door and said, "Honey, someone has sent you some beautiful flowers." As he walked back into the room I asked, "Who sent them?" He'd forgotten to look. He went back and read your card. Son, he has been sitting in his chair for twenty minutes weeping. He was so blessed by the flowers you sent, and what you wrote to him, that he plans to call you and talk with you as soon as he can pull himself together.'"

A few weeks later Michael and his parents spent their first Christmas together in years. In almost no time, Michael and his dad were once again close friends. They forgave each other for past offenses and experienced a wonderful reconciliation.

Michael's father passed away a few years later, and to this day Michael thinks about how he almost missed those years of friendship with his dad. Sending the flowers was a stitch to close the wound in their relationship.

When we turn the word *forgive* around, we get the words "give for." You are well on your way to forgiving when you are willing to *give for* the one who has offended you. This is exactly what God did for us.[5]

MEDICATE THE WOUND

Let's look at a few passages that offer healing for the heart.

Most of all be warm in your love for one another; because in love there is forgiveness for sins without number. (1 Peter 4:8 BBE)

Walk in love, which is the bond of perfection. (Colossians 3:14 WEB)

[A religious scholar asked,] "Teacher, which command in God's Law is the most important?"

Jesus said, "'Love the Lord your God with all your passion and prayer and intelligence.' This is the most important, the first on any list. But there is a second to set alongside it:

'Love others as well as you love yourself'" (Matthew 22: 36–39 THE MESSAGE).

In Luke 10, Jesus tells of a man accosted by thieves on his way to the city of Jericho; the Samaritan who found him along the roadside bound his wounds with oil and wine. (In biblical times, these were used medicinally to prevent infection.) Once your wounds have been cleansed *and* closed, healing can begin.

Dr. Jesus' prescription for the healing of your wounded heart calls for *regular applications of love and prayer* over an extended period of time: "Love your enemies. . . . Pray for those who despitefully use you and persecute you" (Matthew 5:44 MKJV). The enemy has no antidote for these two powerful weapons! As long as you are doing them, the healing process *is* being activated and your pain *will* fade. One day only a scar will remain, a badge of honor, a symbol of your victory over unforgiveness!

HOW BEST TO *GET EVEN*

A kindly old skycap, assisting a wealthy passenger as he checked in for his flight to New York City, accidentally dropped and scratched a piece of the man's expensive luggage.

Though the mishap was completely unintentional, the man began screaming obscenities at the skycap for his apparent carelessness.

The old skycap never looked up. Unfazed, he simply continued to check the man's identification, tag his bags, and process his boarding pass.

Once the awkward and unpleasant encounter ended, the next passenger in line stepped up. "Sir," he said to the elderly servant. "I want to commend you for the patience and self-control I just witnessed. It was perfectly obvious that you didn't intentionally drop that man's luggage. I feel he was totally out of order to scream at you as he did. And I find it remarkable that you didn't attempt to retaliate in any way."

Continuing diligently with his work, the old skycap replied dryly, "Well, I wouldn't say that. You see, he's going to New York City. But his luggage is on its way to the Bahamas."

This story, although it doesn't promote healing (and is *not* the best way to get even), does show that there is usually more than one way to settle the score with those who offend us. When we withhold forgiveness in order to get even, we are rendering evil for evil, and, as we have learned, we actually end up hurting ourselves. The truth is, we can never truly get even the world's way; we only plunge ourselves into deeper bondage.

> *The Yanomano people of Venezuela were a fierce people. Although they were short in stature, they were fierce in battle.*
>
> *One of the ancient customs of this indigenous Venezuelan tribe was to always "get even." Whenever there was a death among their people, the shaman would seek the spirits (evil) and find out who had cursed them. Immediately the men would plan a strategy and in the night the offended tribesmen would stalk into the camp of their enemy and club a woman, child, or baby to death.*
>
> *This was their way to achieve revenge. Yet in the revealing story of* Jungleman, *the old shaman of the Yanomanos stated how he hated the life of his people because the evil spirits would torment them after every act of vengeful death.*[6]

Okay, I admit it: I *always* get even with anyone who offends me. How? By recognizing that Jesus shed His blood and died on Calvary's cross to pay for their sins—including their offenses against me. They are entirely paid for!

What about you? Is there any person (living or dead) who has offended you? Someone with whom you wish to get even? If so, stick with me—I'm writing this chapter especially to you.

Perhaps it has been difficult for you to forgive others because you've embraced an identity of victimhood. *You feel that somebody owes you.* I've suffered my share of offenses at the hands of others through the years. I know what it is to be mistreated, betrayed, and abused. But I assure you that I too had to cancel those kinds of contracts. No one owes me anything. I've marked all those accounts "paid in full by the blood of Jesus." Status: *ACCOUNT CLOSED.* I refuse to be a victim when my Bible says,

> *Do you think anyone is going to be able to drive a wedge between us and Christ's love for us? There is no way! Not trouble, not hard times, not hatred, not hunger, not homelessness, not bullying threats, not backstabbing, not even the worst sins listed in Scripture:*
>
> *They kill us in cold blood because they hate you. We're sitting ducks; they pick us off one by one.*
>
> *None of this fazes us because Jesus loves us. I'm absolutely convinced that nothing—nothing living or dead, angelic or demonic, today or tomorrow, high or low, thinkable or unthinkable—absolutely nothing can get between us and God's love because of the way that Jesus our Master has embraced us.*
> (Romans 8:35–39 THE MESSAGE)

Understand, I'm not letting those who have offended me go free. Oh no! I'm releasing them to Jesus, and *I'm* choosing to go free!—free from unforgiveness, free from resentment, free from bitterness, free from hatred, and, best of all, free from the tormentors. Life is too short for me to rent out that kind of space in my mind or heart.

Some people refuse to forgive others because they sub-consciously feel that to do so would be tantamount to mini-mizing, condoning, or even overlooking the offense. That seems honest enough on the surface, but remember that *God neither discounted nor overlooked our sin in order to save us.* Had He discounted it, or overlooked it in the least, God would have sinned. *Jesus first had to pay for our sin.* When our sin account had been paid in full, *only then could the Father forgive us.*

WAS IT GRACE OR JUSTICE THAT SAVED ME?

> *Forgiveness is the fragrance that the violet sheds on the heel that has crushed it.* (Mark Twain)

We were charged with sin. Heaven's Almighty Judge heard the evidence against us, banged the gavel, and pronounced us "guilty as charged." Then, as required by law, He sentenced us to death. But something utterly amazing occurred!

Jesus stepped down from the Judge's bench, took off His robe of justice, received an unimaginably abusive beating, and carried His cross to the top of Golgatha where He was exe-cuted like a common criminal in our place. Christ's sacrificial death for us was truly an act of grace.

Even so, in the Crucifixion, God ingeniously blended His justice with His grace. When we received Christ as Lord and Savior, both grace and justice were applied—*grace* because we don't deserve God's pardon for our sin, and *justice* because in the very act of pardoning us, God puts into effect the judg-ment He exacted on His son at Calvary.

Remarkably, in saving us, God's grace becomes justice, and God's justice becomes grace. And there are no exceptions, for God has struck a covenant with man and, by His Word, has bound himself to keep it. Without exception, all who surrender to Christ as Lord and Savior will experience both grace and justice in the pardon they receive from God.

Just as God recognized Christ's death in payment for my sin, I also recognize His death on the cross in payment for any offense that someone commits against me. He died for the sins of the world; *that's* how we get even! The blood of God's Son balances the account, and to demand anything else is to demand double jeopardy (illegally requiring two penalties or payments for the same crime).

From this moment on, you will know that refusing to forgive someone is not only a sin against that person, it is also a sin against the blood of Jesus. You are in effect saying, "I know that Jesus died for your sin against me, but you still owe me. You must make additional payment."

Are you harboring unforgiveness toward anyone today? Is there bitterness or resentment in your heart? In our final chapter, when we take our steps to freedom, I'm going to ask you to list those who've offended you and to repent and receive God's forgiveness for failing to forgive them. Then God is going to show you how to love them with your heart, bless them with your words, do good to them with your hands, and pray for them from your spirit!

INSTALLING LOVE

Tech Support: Yes, ma'am, how can I help you?

Customer: Well, I've been having glitches and difficulties, and I've been strongly advised to install Love. Can you guide me through the process?

Tech Support: Yes, I can help you. Are you ready to proceed?

Customer: I'm not very technical, but I'll give it a try. What do I do first?

Tech Support: The first step is to open your heart drive. Have you located your heart drive, ma'am?

Customer: Yes, but wait—several other programs are running right now. Is it okay to install Love while they're running?

Tech Support: Which programs are running?

Customer: Let's see . . . Past-Hurt, Low-Self-Image, Grudge, and Resentment at the moment.

Tech Support: Love will gradually erase Past-Hurt from your current operating system. It may remain in your permanent memory, but it will no longer disrupt other programs. Love will eventually override Low-Self-Image with a module of its own, called Self-Acceptance. However, you will have to completely turn off Grudge and Resentment. Those programs prevent Love from being installed properly. Can you turn those off, ma'am?

Customer: I don't know how. Can you explain?

Tech Support: Yes. Go to your Start menu and invoke Forgiveness. You may have to perform this operation repeatedly before Grudge and Resentment have been completely erased.

Customer: Okay, the process is underway—Love has started installing itself. Is that normal?

Tech Support: Yes, but remember that you only have the *base program*. You will need to begin connecting to other hearts in order to get needed upgrades.

Customer: Okay, I understand. Hey—my heart drive is filling up with new files already!

Tech Support: Good. The system will overwrite any conflicting files and begin to patch faulty programming. Also, you need to delete Self-Criticism from all directories and empty your recycle bin to make sure it's not only completely gone but also never comes back.

Customer: Got it. Smile is playing on my monitor, and Peace and Contentment are copying themselves all over my heart drive. Is *this* normal?

Tech Support: It happens sometimes, yes. Sometimes it takes a while, but eventually everything gets downloaded.

So Love is installed and running? One more thing, then, before we hang up: Love is *freeware*. It was purchased for you many, many years ago. Be sure to give it and its various modules to everyone you meet. They will in turn share it with others and return cool modules back to you.

Customer: I will do just that. By the way, what's your name?

Tech Support: Call me the Divine Cardiologist, the Great Physician, or just "I AM." Most people feel all they need is an annual checkup to stay heart-healthy; but the manufacturer (*Me*) suggests a daily maintenance schedule for maximum Love efficiency on the heart drive. Please contact me *any* time for *any* reason.[7]

Do you remember in Luke 17:5-6 when Jesus' disciples asked him, "Lord, increase our faith?" Obviously they were facing a monumental challenge, which they didn't feel qualified to handle. However, their request for increased faith wasn't in the context of trying to cast out a demon, work a miracle, or even raise the dead. No. They asked Jesus to increase their faith in response to the new instruction he had given them to forgive others. There are few things more challenging than this! I pray that God will increase your faith.

CHAPTER SEVEN

Making Things Right

As my dad, Pastor Robert Smith, left for his office one morning, he looked over his shoulder and said, "Eddie, when you get home from school today, please mow the lawn for me." I nodded in agreement, although my sixteen-year-old brain was hardly engaged at that early hour.

Sure enough, later that day when I arrived home, I immediately constructed a towering peanut butter and jelly sandwich, poured myself a tall glass of cold milk, and took my usual semi-conscious position in the den in front of the television to watch cartoons.

Somehow, distantly, while watching Popeye, Olive, and Bluto, I heard my father's car approaching. You can always hear a preacher's car pull into the driveway!

I heard the car door close, heard him enter the house, and moments later heard him in the garage starting the lawn-mower. I was still mentally lost in Cartoon Land.

But suddenly, as though a bucket of icy water had been

poured on my head, it dawned on me: *He's mowing the lawn!*

I leaped from the recliner, rushed to the front door, and looked out across the yard. There was my dad, in his now sweaty work clothes, doing my job. I thought to myself, *He's been working all day. Now he comes home to find that I haven't done the only thing he asked me to do.* I was both embarrassed and ashamed. Finally I mustered enough courage to step outside. As he turned the corner, I slipped up beside him. He moved aside and allowed me to take the mower, and I finished the job.

―――――――――

Later, at the dinner table, my two brothers were eating as if food was going to be removed from the grocers' shelves the next day. I was unusually quiet, my head was hung, and I was pushing a pea around with my knife, making grease circles on my plate.

Noticing, Dad asked, "Eddie, are you all right? Is something wrong?"

After a moment I said, "Yes sir, something *is* wrong. Would you forgive me for not mowing the lawn like you asked me to this morning?"

Dad lowered his head, looked over the top of his glasses, and smiled. "Forgive you? Why, son, I already have." With those words a huge load of guilt was lifted off my shoulders.

There is something very important you must understand about this story: I didn't have to confess my sin to my father in order to *be* forgiven. As he said, he'd already forgiven me. The guilt I was feeling was legitimate and it brought me face to face with Dad to deal with the matter, but it wasn't an issue in my father's heart—he'd already removed my guilt. I only needed to confess in order to *experience* his forgiveness for me.

The same is true with our heavenly Father, who through the finished work of His Son fully paid the price for our sin.

Then why does 1 John 1:9 instruct us to confess our sin? Once we've received eternal life, we confess our sins to Him in order to maintain our fellowship with Him. Otherwise, while others are enjoying God's abundance, we'll find ourselves spiritually pushing peas and making grease circles.

Complete and effective confession of sin means more than admitting we've sinned. It means agreeing with God concerning our sin, *seeing our sins from God's perspective.* Full confession is applying (in our own hearts and minds) what God has done with our sin and guilt. This is accomplished in the following manner.

BE SPECIFIC REGARDING YOUR SINS

When you wash your clothing at home, you don't cram the laundry bag into the machine. You'd never get your clothes clean that way. First, you empty the bag, then you place each piece into the washing machine, individually.

Likewise, with confession: Praying "God forgive me of all my sins" is like stuffing the whole hamper into the washer. Instead, take each sin and confess it to the Lord, and ask Him for His peace. To completely confess your sins, you must be willing to face them *specifically,* one by one.

AGREE WITH GOD CONCERNING THE SEVERITY OF YOUR SIN

Some of us have conveniently categorized "types" of sin in order to make allowances in our lives. *After all,* we reason, *a little white lie is not as serious as a big black one.* But it makes no difference to God—all lying is sin.

Some rationalize that drunkenness is a disease; the Bible calls it sin. Others conclude that homosexuality, which God calls "vile affections," and for which He utterly destroyed the city of Sodom, is simply an alternative lifestyle. Some call fornicating "living together."[1] Others say that lusting really isn't a big deal, yet Christ said, "I tell you that everyone who gazes at a woman to lust after her has committed adultery with her already in his heart" (Matthew 5:27–28 HNV).

Hey, our holy God has a zero-tolerance policy when it comes to sin. The fact that we can and do make peace with our sin should concern us. God loves sinners as much as He hates sin, but our sin is a wedge separating us from Him. To completely confess our sins, *we must also agree with God concerning their severity.* Besides, sin not only destroys our fellowship with God and our effectiveness in His kingdom, it will eventually destroy our mental and physical health as well.

ACKNOWLEDGE YOUR SINS

The psalmist wrote, "I acknowledged my sin unto thee, and mine iniquity have I not hid. I said, I will confess my transgressions unto the LORD; and thou forgavest the iniquity of my sin" (32:5). Some of us are masters at rationalizing our sins and justifying ourselves. We find it difficult to face the fruit of our sin nature.

Many years ago I was invited to the home of a pastor friend. We were enjoying a delicious Sunday lunch with his family, when his precious yet precocious five-year-old daughter finished eating and asked to be excused early. She left, and when the rest of us were done, we retired to the living room, where I noticed my sunglasses laying on the recliner . . . in pieces. Completely crushed! I immediately knew what had happened.

I called the little girl over and asked lovingly, "Marylou, did you sit on my glasses?"

She dropped her head, sulked a bit, and answered, "No sir."

I pressed a bit further. "Marylou, did you *accidentally* sit on them?"

With guilt written all over her cute little face, she diverted her eyes and again answered no.

"Are you sure you didn't *mistakenly* sit on my sunglasses?"

At that, her tiny voice broke: "I . . . I . . . I *almost* did."

Just like some of us, Marylou just couldn't bring herself to face what she had done. To completely confess your sin, you must be willing to *acknowledge your sin* and admit that you are indeed a sinner.

RECEIVE YOUR CLEANSING

On Easter Sunday when our youngest son, Bryan, was five, we dressed him in his new little white suit, shirt, and tie to match. We laced up his new white patent leather shoes and instructed him to sit on the porch like a gentleman while we dressed for church; the lawn was soaked from an overnight rain.

Alice was still putting the finishing touches to her makeup, when I looked out the living room window and saw something that left me aghast: Bryan had made himself at home in a puddle. He was covered with mud from head to toe.

After our initial panic had subsided, we brought Bryan inside, bathed him, and then dressed him in his usual Sunday attire. Did we forgive him? Sure we did. But we also had to clean him up before we could take him to church.

> *If we admit our sins—make a clean breast of them—he won't let us down; he'll be true to himself. He'll forgive our sins and purge us of all wrongdoing.* (1 John 1:9 THE MESSAGE)

God forgives us when we confess. But that's not all: *He cleanses us of all unrighteousness* and pronounces us "not guilty."

RECEIVE YOUR FORGIVENESS

Forgiveness was available to both of the thieves who were crucified alongside Jesus. However, one thief received Christ's forgiveness, the other didn't. Only one is in heaven with Him today; the other thief will be in torment forever. After this life, there are no second chances—hell has no fire exit.[2]

It's sad that some Christians struggle to forgive others. Sadder still are those who cannot forgive themselves for past sins, choosing to live under an unnecessary cloud of false, self-imposed guilt that spiritually sabotages them. Part of confessing our sin is actually *receiving God's forgiveness*.

AGREE WITH GOD ABOUT WHAT HE'S DONE WITH YOUR SINS

God didn't *only* forgive our sins; excusing our sins would have made Him a sinner. God's grace was not an act of *overlooking* our sin; instead, He took the punishment himself, paying our sin-debt in full. (Excuse me a moment while I shout!)

We must realize that "He loved us, and sent his Son to be the propitiation for our sins" (1 John 4:10). That word *propitiation* is amazing. Get this: It literally means that *Christ's death on the cross calmed God's outraged holiness on our account*. We chose to sin against God, and our sin cost Him the life of His sinless Son, the sacrificial Lamb who died in our place. Salvation is free, but it's certainly not cheap—the ultimate price was paid for us.

Now I'll show my age. When I was in elementary school, we didn't have Wite-Out™ to correct our written mistakes. We had "ink eradicator." At least that's what it was called; in actuality, it was a little bottle of chlorine bleach with a glass dauber.

When I made an error with my fountain pen (this was before the advent of ballpoints), I would dip the glass dauber into the ink eradicator and then wipe it on the mistake. It didn't cover the fault (like Wite-Out does)—it literally bleached the ink's color off the page. Eradicated: not covered, but *gone*.

In the Old Testament when people put their trust in God, their sins were *covered*. For example, in Psalm 32:1, David wrote, "Blessed is he whose transgression is forgiven, whose sin is covered." It is as though Old Testament saints were saved "on credit," awaiting God's ultimate payment for their sin. Every sacrificial lamb that was slain was metaphorically like the swipe of a spiritual credit card; it was an obedient expression of the faith of God's people. The writer of Hebrews declares, however, "It is impossible for the blood of bulls and goats to take away sins" (10:4 NIV).

At long last, on Calvary, Jesus paid off their account balance—and ours! "He did not enter by means of the blood of goats and calves; but he entered the Most Holy Place once for all by his own blood, having obtained eternal redemption" (Hebrews 9:12 NIV).

When Jesus appeared to John the Baptist, John announced His arrival as "the Lamb of God who takes away the sin of the world."[3] You see, if an innocent sin-bearer were all that was needed, Jesus could have died for us at birth—our sin would already have been atoned for, and we would be made innocent (cleansed). But this is not all that was needed, for righteousness is more than innocence: *Righteousness means "having overcome sin."*

Jesus had to live His life, confront and be confronted by Satan, be tempted as we are, and overcome sin at every turn in order to become righteous.

Christ became righteous through His obedience. When we receive Him, God not only eradicates (takes away) our sin, He applies Christ's righteousness to our account. (See 2 Corinthians 5:21.)

After Jesus had given His life, ascended into heaven, and applied His blood to the mercy seat, sins were no longer covered;[4] we are now *cleansed* from our sin. "If we confess our sins, he is faithful and just to forgive us our sins, and to cleanse us from all unrighteousness" (1 John 1:9). You might uncover something that is covered, but you cannot locate something that has been eradicated. (By the way, neither can Satan.)

On one occasion in the early 1970s, Alice and I were conducting an outdoor revival meeting in rural Louisiana. In those days, many rural southern churches would have "brush-arbor revival meetings" every spring. The old-timers would dump sawdust on the ground, drive loose nails back into the old pine benches, and spread brush atop the overhead arbor.

(In fact, it was at one of those brush-arbor revivals that I was born again.

While giving my testimony one night, I lightheartedly said, "When I was five and one-half years of age, I was saved from a life of crime and drug abuse."

After the service, a distinguished-looking lady courteously approached and asked, "Did I hear you say that you were involved with crime and drug abuse when you were only five and a half?"

"No, ma'am," I clarified. "I said that I was saved *from* a life of crime and drug abuse. And God alone knows what else I have been and am being saved *from!*")

Anyway—back to my story—I was that week's preacher at the brush-arbor revival, and one night I said, "Who would like to share a word of testimony?"

A young teenage "preacher boy" enthusiastically raised his hand. (You can always tell a preacher boy—you just can't tell him much.) I invited him to the front and handed him the microphone, which he was clearly anxious to get his hands on. He rolled back the cover of his Bible—as he'd no doubt seen his favorite evangelist do—thrust it into the air above his head, and began to preach with gusto.

"The Bible says that every sin you've ever committed has been captured on film. And one day, when we get to heaven, a giant screen will come down. God's projector will begin to roll, and the film of your life will be projected for everyone to see, including everything you've done in darkness, as well as every sin you've ever committed—"

I gently tapped him on the shoulder, and he paused. "Sir?" he asked.

I quietly said, "Son, you can go back to your seat now."

"But sir," he insisted. "I'm not finished."

"You may not be finished, son," I explained kindly, "but you are through."

As he returned to his seat, I explained. "Folks, I don't honestly know whether or not God has taken a film of my life. The Bible certainly doesn't say that He has. Furthermore, I don't know if there is a giant screen in heaven or even a heavenly projector. But I do know one thing for sure: If all of that *is* true, the film of my life has been edited by the blood of His Son, Jesus."

There is not one frame that would embarrass me. *Not one sin can be found.* I find great consolation in Isaiah 43:25 (NKJV), where God says, "I, even I, am He who blots out your trespasses for My own sake; and I will not remember your sins." I especially like *The Message* rendering: "But I, yes I, am the one who takes care of your sins—that's what I do. I don't keep a list of your sins." Hallelujah!

That's what makes God's salvation so great. He eradicates our sin! Complete confession means more than admitting that we are guilty; it is *agreeing with God about what He's done with our sin.* That, my friend, is absolute victory!

CHAPTER EIGHT

Shedding My Graveclothes

What could Jesus expect? He knew full well what He had to do: return to Judea, where the Jews were waiting to kill Him. And if that weren't enough, Jesus was going to challenge death, just as He had already done in Nain with the widow's son.[1]

His close friend Lazarus, Mary and Martha's brother, had already lain dead in the tomb for four days. Those who knew said the stench of decaying flesh was already prominent. Just thinking about it broke Jesus' heart.

When He arrived, the family of the deceased led Him to the little hillside cave. Once there, Jesus had them remove the stone slab that covered the opening. He looked up to heaven, thanked the Father for always hearing Him, then shouted boldly, "Lazarus, come out!"

Immediately, to everyone's absolute amazement, they heard a rustling inside. Then Lazarus, who by now seemed to be little more than a wrapped-up cadaver, stumbled out of the darkness into the bright sunlight.

Jesus said, "Unwrap him and let him loose." Many of the Jews who witnessed the miracle believed in Him.[2]

Astonishing! One moment, Lazarus was dead . . . and the next, he was fully alive. This story is a wonderful illustration of our new-birth experience. One minute we were spiritually dead in our trespasses and sins;[3] a moment later, we were fully alive in Christ.[4] Phenomenal!

Can you imagine how exciting it must have been to watch Lazarus exit that tomb after having lain dead for four days? Now, Lazarus was indeed alive. But if he was to enjoy and effectively live his new life, one more thing was necessary: the graveclothes that he wore in death had to be removed. I'm writing this to you so that today you can be freed from your *spiritual* graveclothes.[5] Only then will you be free to truly enjoy your new life and live it effectively for God's glory.

It's one thing for God to forgive us, cleanse us, and breathe into us His eternal life. (That's the new birth.) It's another thing altogether for us to remove the graveclothes, things that relate to our former lives when we were dead in trespasses and sins. We may be spiritually alive in Christ, but if we remain wrapped in the clothes of spiritual death, we'll continually struggle with satanic accusation and self-condemnation. This is a matter of deliverance from an old mindset to a new one.

DELIVERANCE

God's deliverance is the outworking of justification and sanctification in our lives. From the moment we're born again, we're continually being delivered from unbiblical thinking, from the sinful habits of our former lifestyles, and even from the attachments any evil spirits might have to us, whether from generational sins, our own acts of disobedience, or trauma we've experienced.

The United States is one of the few nations on earth where Christians are seldom brought through personal deliverance once they've been reborn. In most developing nations, converts to Christianity today are usually first-generation believers whose parents and grandparents worshiped idols (demon gods). For them, deliverance is presumed to be an elemental first step after coming to Christ, a foundational preparation for living the Christian life. Don't forget that it was Jesus' faithful follower Mary Magdalene, "out of whom he had cast seven devils," to whom He revealed himself first on His resurrection morning.[6]

In the early 1990s, a couple of years after the Soviet Union collapsed, Alice and I were ministering in Riga, the capital of Latvia. On one bitterly cold and snowy Sunday night, we decided to visit one of the city's fastest-growing churches.

The evening service was packed with Latvians and Russians. We sat bundled up in every article of warm clothing we had; as was common at that time, there was no heating in public buildings. But that didn't cool down the fiery passion and hunger for God among those several thousand people. At the conclusion of the invitation, almost fifty received salvation at the altar.

The next step was one we should adopt in the U.S. The pastor had the new believers turn and face the crowd. He led them to corporately renounce their old lives of sin, all occult and cultic involvement, and all associations with evil spirits; then he led them in a commitment to follow Christ in believer's baptism, to be faithful to the fellowship of believers, to tithe on their incomes, and to walk in accountability. God was glorified that night!

Have you ever truly considered how lost you were when Christ found you? In Ephesians 2:1–3 (NIV), Paul writes:

> *You were dead in your transgressions and sins, in which you used to live when you followed the ways of this world and of the ruler of the kingdom of the air, the spirit who is now at work in those who are disobedient. All of us also lived among them at one time, gratifying the cravings of our sinful nature and following its desires and thoughts. Like the rest, we were by nature objects of wrath.*

When we sin, we cooperate with the enemy and open doors to him. It's one thing for God to forgive our sins, which He does when we confess them. However, it's another thing for us to close the doors that we've opened to darkness and take back the ground that we've given the devil. When we do this, we are enforcing God's law against the lawless one; we are canceling those lingering contracts with darkness that we have ignored. They are what have empowered Satan to harass us.

SELF-SABOTAGE!

I'm a PK (preacher's kid) who was saved at a very young age. From that moment I knew God had cleansed me and forgiven me of my sins. I'd even memorized the verses. But it didn't take long for me to realize that born-again Christians also sin. Through the years I've failed the Lord on many occasions. Confessing sin is more than a doctrine—it's my practice.[7]

As we have seen, Revelation 12:10 says Satan is our accuser, and he certainly wasted no time accusing me. Even after I became a minister, the devil would war against my mind, assaulting me with things like, "What about *that sin* you committed when you were thirteen?"

On these occasions, I would know that God had cleansed and forgiven me for that sin, but I wouldn't know what to do to stop Satan's accusing voice. And when *he* wasn't accusing me, I found myself entertaining self-condemning thoughts. I couldn't seem to forgive myself for sins I'd committed. The self-condemnation only fueled my mental torment: *self-sabotage*. I was told to take those thoughts captive and bring them under the obedience of Christ;[8] however, constantly wrestling with them in my own strength took my focus off of God, consumed my energy, and kept me from attaining higher heights and deeper depths with Christ.

I knew things were right in heaven, yet when I told the accuser that my sins were forgiven, he refused to listen. Now I know why: he still held the contracts that I'd signed in my sin, the original agreements that had opened the door and allowed him legal right to my life. He was standing on ground I'd deeded to him! Because *I* had yielded that ground, *I* was the one who would have to destroy the contracts and take it back.

One glorious day God showed me how to pull the rug out from under the enemy's feet. Upon learning this, I tore up the contracts, took back the territory, and summarily dismissed the devil. *It was awesome!*

Perhaps you too were taught not to look back at your past—especially to sins committed before you were saved. You were promised that God had cleansed you from those sins, had graciously taken them as far as the east is from the west, and would never remember them against you again.[9]

All of this is true. We *are* new creations. We *have* been forgiven for past sins.[10] But there is more to this issue of our former sins than how they affect our relationship with God. *How they affect us is also important,* as is how they affect the kingdom of darkness. We dare not overlook this.

FALSE GUILT

The blood of Jesus has removed the guilt of my sins forever.[11] But again, I'm not talking about *real* guilt; I'm talking about *false* guilt in the forms of satanic accusation and self-condemnation.

Yes, God no longer remembers the sins you've confessed, but *you* remember them, and the devil will take advantage of that. Satan and his evil minions will use anything they can to keep you beaten down. They will use everything from *It's been two days since you've read your Bible—how can you call yourself a Christian?* to *Sure, you've asked God to forgive your adultery, but you can never make it up to Him or to your spouse. You're a loser—face it, God will never be able to use you.* If you're being victimized by these kinds of thoughts, consider the following story:

> Little Johnny, *visiting his grandparents' farm, was given a slingshot to play with in the woods. He practiced, but he could never hit a target. He was deeply discouraged when he headed back to the house for dinner.*
>
> *As he walked the path, he noticed his grandmother's pet duck. Impulsively, he aimed his slingshot and released a stone; the duck was hit square in the head and died instantly.*
>
> *Johnny was shocked and grieved.* He hadn't meant to do it. *In a panic, he hid the duck in the woodpile . . . only then to see his sister watching. Sally had observed it all, but she said nothing.*
>
> *After dinner that night, when Grandma said, "Sally, let's wash the dishes," Sally replied, "Grandma, Johnny told me he wanted to help in the kitchen." Then she leaned over and whispered, "Johnny, remember the duck?" So Johnny did the dishes.*
>
> *The next day, when Grandpa asked if the children wanted to go fishing, Grandma said, "I'm sorry, but I need Sally to help me prepare dinner." Sally grinned. "Grandma, Johnny*

told me that he wanted to help prepare dinner." She whispered again, "Remember the duck?" So Sally went fishing, and Johnny stayed to help Grandma.

    After several days of doing both his and Sally's chores, Johnny finally couldn't stand it any longer. He went to Grandma and tearfully confessed what he'd done. She knelt down, gave him a hug, and said, "Sweetheart, I know. I was standing at the window, and I saw the whole thing. Because I love you, I forgave you. I was just wondering how long you'd let Sally make a slave of you."

Perhaps you can identify with Johnny. No matter what past sins you've confessed that the enemy keeps throwing in your face—lying, fornication, fear, rebellion, hatred, anger, addiction, unforgiveness, stealing, adultery, abortion, drunkenness, or anything else—you need to know that Jesus was standing at the window. He witnessed the whole thing. He loves you. He has cleansed and forgiven you. *He's just wondering how long you'll needlessly allow Satan to enslave you.*

CHAPTER NINE

Making Restitution: When Repenting Isn't Enough

Repentance has become a lost art in American society. Almost daily we hear high-profile people, caught in crimes, attempt to justify or excuse themselves rather than take responsibility for their actions. They usually squeeze out a confession to having "made a mistake," but few say—as my friend Jim Bakker said, following his much-publicized failure—*"I was wrong."* Repentance is vital if we are to maintain our moral compass and live in fellowship with a holy God and with one another. Nevertheless, there are times when even repentance isn't enough.

In times of true revival, I've seen people do remarkable things. While making peace with her past, one woman remembered stealing a pacifier from a druggist's shelf when she was only nine. Why? Because she and a neighborhood friend thought it would be cool to play with pacifiers one afternoon. Decades later, the Lord brought this sin to mind; it was a hole in her armor that the devil could use to accuse her. So the next day God asked her to write a letter of apology to the druggist.

> *Dear Sir,*
>
> *Many years ago, when I was nine years old, I stole a baby pacifier from your store to play with. I am so sorry. Please forgive me. Enclosed is $25 to cover the cost of the pacifier, plus interest. I wish to close this open account. Thank you.*
>
>

Sincerely,

Name Withheld
>

Did the druggist really care about the missing pacifier? Of course he didn't, prompting some to ask, "What's the point?" The issue wasn't that the druggist was offended—he didn't even know what had happened. Nor was it about God's forgiveness—that too was settled. It was about this woman's own peace of mind, about her being reconciled with her past, and about her making restitution. *It was about closing a hole in her armor so she could be free from satanic accusation and self-condemnation in the future.* Understand, she was taking to heart Ephesians 4:27, where Paul warns, "Don't give the Devil . . . [a] foothold in your life" (THE MESSAGE). Or, as the *Contemporary English Version* reads, "Don't give the devil a chance."

THE LITTLE BIG MAN

Do you remember this story from the gospel of Luke?

> *Jesus entered Jericho and began to walk through the city. A rich man there, Zacchaeus, the head tax collector, wanted desperately to see Jesus. Problem was, the crowd interfered—he was a short man and couldn't see over them. So he ran on ahead,*

climbing up a sycamore tree in order to see Jesus when He came by.

As Jesus approached, he looked up and said, "Zacchaeus, hurry down. Today I'll be a guest in your home." Zacchaeus scrambled to the ground, hardly believing his good luck but delighted to take Jesus home with him. Some who saw the incident were indignant and grumped, "What business does Jesus have getting cozy with this crook?"

But Zacchaeus, a little stunned, stood up and stammered apologetically: "Master, I will immediately give away half my income to the poor—and if there's anyone I've cheated, I'll pay four times the damages."

Jesus replied, "Today is salvation day in this home; here he is, Zacchaeus, son of Abraham! For the Son of Man came to find and restore the lost" (Luke 19:1–10, paraphrased).

Zacchaeus, the wealthy tax man, who'd unscrupulously taken advantage of others to make his fortune, was ready to give half his wealth to the poor and repay—up to four times—anyone he had cheated. That's more than "Sorry, I made a mistake." It's also a great deal more than repentance. *It's the biblical principle of restitution,* and it's the attitude of one truly seeking the favor of Jesus.

Where did Zacchaeus get such an idea? Perhaps it was from Old Testament passages like this one:

A thief must make full restitution for what is stolen. The thief who is unable to pay is to be sold for his thieving. If caught red-handed with the stolen goods, and the ox or donkey or lamb is still alive, the thief pays double.

If someone grazes livestock in a field or vineyard but lets them loose so they graze in someone else's field, restitution must be made from the best of the owner's field or vineyard.

If fire breaks out and spreads to the brush so that the

sheaves of grain or the standing grain or even the whole field is burned up, whoever started the fire must pay for the damages. (Exodus 22:3–6 THE MESSAGE)

A twenty-first-century story can also paint a clear picture. Bob (not his real name) was a dear friend of ours who once owned a large business. He worked sacrificially to make it successful, and succeed he did—in his business's glory days, Bob supported missionaries and evangelists all over the world.

However, due to a national economic downturn, the day came when Bob's business was no longer lucrative. Finally, to his sorrow, he was forced to declare bankruptcy. Even so, for Bob (unlike with a growing number of overextended Americans), bankruptcy wasn't a way to get out of debt. Rather, it was an available legal option that could protect what was truly his and protect his family from the harassment of angry creditors.

As soon as the bankruptcy was complete, Bob, who'd been a corporate executive and business owner, applied for a menial job. Month after month, year after year, Bob and his dear wife (who also worked) took every available dollar and paid off the business debt—$180,000. Bob considered the debt a moral responsibility, disregarding that legally he wasn't required to repay one cent.

I will never forget the day, more than a decade later, when Bob called to say he was sending a check for $287 to close the last remaining past-due account. Bob was a man of integrity, a man of his word. Bob took his commitments seriously for the gospel's sake; to his eternal credit, he made restitution.

While Bob's need to make restitution was not due to any personal sin, in many cases (as in the example of Zacchaeus), our need for restitution is indeed a result of our sin.

WHAT IS RESTITUTION?

In the church today, few Christian principles are more overlooked than restitution, which means *to restore or to repay an equivalent of what was lost or taken*. What about you? Do you have past issues requiring restitution? Do you owe someone you haven't repaid (and are not repaying)? Think back. Ever move out of an apartment for which you still owed rent? Stiff your roommate for a phone or utility bill? Leave a state without taking care of a traffic fine or parking ticket? Fail to make good on a personal loan from a parent or friend?

I never cease to be amazed at how many people's finances are cursed through defiance or ignorance of this vital principle. If you have unresolved issues like these in your past, you have holes in your armor through which the devil can (and will) accuse you. Making restitution closes those holes. Remember, our purpose is to glorify God in all things, to be reconciled with God and others, and to remove any remnant of the past that gives the enemy ground for his accusations.

Eighteen-year-old Kenneth left home after high school to make his mark on the world. The trouble was, as was the case with many of us, the world made its mark on him. He ended up a bit of a prodigal, but after a few years he returned to straighten out his life and serve Christ, which he has done wonderfully.

The first week Kenneth was home, his dad had him make a list of everyone he owed. Initially it appeared he didn't owe anyone anything, but then his father began to probe. He asked Kenneth about any rent he'd failed to cover, bills he'd walked away from, fines he'd never paid, and so on. His response was, "Dad, I'll never be able to remember them all." Kenneth's dad told him to remember what he could, and then in the future to write down any others that God brought to mind.

Within three days he'd prepared his list; it was amazing

what the Lord revealed to him. He and his dad sat down together and made a budget. He was to get a job, and every extra dime he made above his tithe and his personal needs would be used to pay off these debts.

Naturally, his first protest was, "Dad, some of these people have already charged this off—they no longer expect me to pay." The father explained to him that this wasn't about the expectations of others; *God* expected him to keep his vows and to pay his bills. This was about closing all his open accounts. This was about his peace of mind, a clear conscience. This was about personal integrity and the freedom to live without future accusation. This was about taking back ground that he'd willingly given to the enemy, who could then build a stronghold from which he could mentally and emotionally accuse. Most of all, this was about glorifying God in all things!

The bottom line: These "open accounts" are essentially the same as stealing a man's wallet, grabbing a woman's purse, or robbing a convenience store. *Theft is theft.* Until we repay what we owe others, we can forget about God's blessing upon our lives.

Understand that I'm not talking about debts that you're faithfully paying off as agreed—that's *legitimate* debt. For example, when you buy an automobile, you have an arranged monthly payment to make; as long as you pay it on time, the debt is serviced, the lender is satisfied, and you're at peace. I'm talking about debts toward which you're not making regular payments—bills you've chalked off, ignored, put in the back of your mind, swept under the carpet, or assumed no longer exist. I'm telling you today that they *do* exist.

Jesus clearly taught that when we come to the altar to bring our offering to God (whether our financial offering or the offering of the fruit of our lips—praise, worship, or prayer), and then remember that we have unreconciled issues with another person, we are to stop! We cannot march into the future with Christ until we have reconciled the past, which often requires restitution. Only after restitution are we to bring our gift to God; otherwise, our gift doesn't honor the Lord.[1] If you aren't working toward fulfilling your end of the bargain, then your lenders have claims on your life, and the contracts you signed with them (written or oral) remain in force. When you're not right with your fellow man, your worship of God is unacceptable.

Any debt that I owe is a claim upon me.
The more claims there are upon me,
the less of me I have to give to God.

For the first several years of our marriage, Alice and I lived in a motor home and traveled from city to city doing evangelism. We had no house or apartment—you could say we lived on a piece of "wheel estate." Our bills were paid, but there was always too much month left at the end of the money, and we were truly struggling financially. No matter how hard we tried, we simply couldn't get ahead.

We decided that the only way to break the back of this financial bondage was to increase our giving. So that year we doubled our tithe: We gave 20 percent of our gross income to the Lord and His work. At the end of the year, to our shock and dismay, we were deeper in debt than ever. So the following year we decided to bite the bullet and triple-tithe, thinking that's what it would take to escape our financial straits. (Parenthetically, we give more than that to other ministries now, but joyfully and without any expectation. Thankfully, we no longer attempt to bribe God!)

One February night during a crusade in a city auditorium in Missouri, I was standing on stage when the Lord pointed out a businessman in the center aisle: *That man has the answer to your problem.* I thought, *How can this man I've never met possibly have the answer to my problem?* However, I was inexpressibly relieved just to hear from God about this issue.

After the service I approached the man and said, "Sir, I don't know you, but I need to make an appointment with you. What is your occupation?"

He said, "I'm an accountant." It all began to make sense; we set the appointment for Thursday morning.

We arrived at his office early, and once we were seated, he asked, "What is your problem?" I explained our financial dilemma, emphasizing how we barely kept our bills paid and how we'd just begun to triple-tithe in order to escape financial bondage.

He asked, "To whom do you owe money?"

I listed all of our creditors and the amounts we were paying.

He said, "This is not what I'm referring to. I'm talking about those things you don't consider a bill. Who is it that you owe that you haven't paid?"

"No one," I replied.

"That's not true."

"Well, there is one thing. When I produced my first album, the recording company overcharged me 100 percent. So I did a little research. When I paid them their costs, plus a reasonable profit, I sent them a letter explaining how they had taken advantage of my inexperience and youth, what I had learned, what I had paid, and that I felt that the balance of the bill was unjust and I didn't plan to pay it."

"How much was left unpaid?" he asked.

"Twenty-five-hundred dollars."

"Did you sign a contract with them for the entire amount?"

"Yes . . . but the contract was unfair."

"Then you must pay the entire amount."

"But they took advantage of me," I argued.

"That has nothing to do with it," he countered. "You should have never signed a contract you felt was unfair. Two wrongs don't make a right! It's a bill you agreed to pay. It will not be settled until you pay it in full. Consider it the price of your education."

"Sir, I can't pay the bills I have, much less this one," I protested. "I'll never be able to pay a $2,500 bill!"

"Pray with me right now," he ordered, "that God will provide $2,500 above and beyond what you expect. And then promise Him that when He does, you will take that $2,500 and pay these people what you owe them."

In one sense I felt relieved, because I knew I would never have an additional $2,500! So I prayed with him . . . and two days later the phone rang. The pastor of a large church in Houston said, "Eddie, we know this is short notice. The singer for our revival is sick—he just called and cancelled. Would you and Alice be able to come lead our music next Monday through Wednesday nights?"

This was in the mid-'70s, when our usual offering would have been $200 to $500, but the pastor came to me at the end of the three-day revival and gave me a check for $2,500. The Lord had answered our prayer! I endorsed it, placed it in an envelope along with a letter of apology and explanation, and mailed it the next morning to the record company. When I did, the curse on our finances was broken. We were amazed at how heaven's windows opened from that day forward, and the peace of God was evident in our lives and on our ministry.

Paul said,

Believe me, I do my level best to keep a clear conscience before God and my neighbors in everything I do. (Acts 24:16 THE MESSAGE)

You may have repented of your sins, but you're still being plagued by them. If you have victimized someone else, you may need to make restitution. You may have lingering debts to repay, people from whom, in one form or another, you have stolen and need to compensate. Perhaps you'll never be able to right every wrong you've committed, but if God continually brings to your attention specific people and incidents from your past, He is urging you to make restitution.

It was said of the Welsh Revival that outstanding debts were being paid by countless young converts and that *restitution* was the order of the day. If you are to experience personal revival, renewal, and restoration, *you may need to go beyond repentance and make restitution*. If this is the case, do it today. The following is based on a true story:

> *Bill and Janet, married for almost twenty-five years, were strong believers with a wonderful Christian marriage and family. But one day their entire world was turned upside down by a surprise guest: Bill's twenty-seven-year-old son, Jack.*
>
> *Before Bill met Janet and before he found Christ, he'd lived a wicked life. Until Jack knocked on their front door that day and introduced himself, Bill had never known that his old girlfriend had become pregnant and given birth to his son.*
>
> *Bill and Janet took Jack into their home. They claimed him as a son, paid for his education, and taught him about Jesus Christ. This is restitution.*

If the person you owe is deceased, then pay his heirs what you owed him. If you can't establish contact with anyone regarding your debt, I suggest you make a charitable donation of that amount to an appropriate nonprofit organization. Don't look for excuses. Take the initiative. It's serious business to be serious about your relationship with God.

CHAPTER TEN

Taking the Steps to Freedom

"Free at last! Free at last!
Thank God Almighty, we are free at last!"
—Negro Spiritual

My daughter Ashlee (about fifteen at the time) and I were in the lobby of the Presidential Hotel in Port Harcourt, Nigeria, waiting for the van that would take us to the convention center, where more than ten thousand people were gathered for the crusade at which I was speaking. The van was late and the weather was unbearably hot, so we walked over to the bar and ordered Cokes.

As we stood there sipping and talking, two beautiful young Nigerian women slipped up beside me. One of them nudged me and quietly said, "Are you lonely?"

Now, I'm no rocket scientist, nor the son of a rocket scientist, but in my years of travel I've learned a few of the world's ways. This young prostitute was attempting to proposition me, right in front of my own daughter.

I smiled and politely answered, "No. I'm *definitely* not lonely."

With a giggle she probed again, and I decided this was an opportunity to present the gospel of Christ.

"Ladies," I began, "do you know about American slavery? Have you heard how your forefathers captured and sold each other to American slave traders who mercilessly caged them, carted them off, and shipped them to my country to suffer in bondage?"

"Yes, I'm familiar with all of that," one of them responded.

"Your African ancestors who were sold into slavery had no choice in the matter. But why have you *chosen* to live as a slave to sin and to Satan?"

"I'm not sure what you mean," she answered. However, the other woman knew exactly what I meant, and she dropped her head in guilt.

I continued to explain how they had opted for slavery. Then I carefully told them of God's love and His gracious offer of salvation. I had just outlined the terms of receiving Christ when the van arrived and we were hurried outside.

"Why don't you ladies climb in with my daughter and me and accompany us to the crusade at the convention center?" I invited. The one who seemed to be hearing the gospel for the first time stepped forward, but the one with the guilt-ridden face held her back. Again I asked and was refused, so Ashlee and I closed the van door and the driver made his way toward the hotel gate.

We had no sooner exited onto the city street than those two women ran up, flagged down the driver, and climbed aboard. You should have seen the faces of God's people as the evangelist and his daughter stepped out of the van with two prime prospects for salvation. We were separated from them in the crowd, but we prayed that the Lord would set them free that night. We trust He did.

FREEDOM FROM FALSE GUILT

As we have learned in the preceding chapters, there's a difference between being set free from the *true guilt of sin,* which is removed by the blood of Jesus, and being set free from *false guilt:* satanic accusation and self-condemnation. By now I'm sure you're anxious to take the steps to freedom, but in order to properly complete the process, you will need the following:

(1) At least an hour of uninterrupted time. Two hours is even better.
(2) A completely private location where you can pray and speak aloud.
(3) A pen and plenty of paper. A legal pad is perfect.

The steps to freedom consist of making lists and taking action. The lists that you make are extremely personal, for your eyes only; you will want to guard them carefully, and as you complete the process, you will completely destroy them.

As uncomfortable as it might seem now, you will soon see that this exercise is a tool with which you can escape Satan's trap once and for all. By the way, don't cheat: Do this thoroughly! Take your time and don't rush. Allow the Holy Spirit to bring key offenses to your mind; remember, these are the graveclothes from which you need to be set free.

Once you've made your lists, you will be going item-by-item through each one, taking specific steps that I will show you. We'll begin when you're ready.

STEP 1: ANCESTRAL INIQUITY

Let's invite the Holy Spirit to guide you in this process. Read this prayer aloud, and feel free to add to it if you are led.

Father in heaven, I come before you now to apply the work of the Cross to my life. I want the new freedom that I am about to receive to glorify your holy name and extend your heavenly kingdom. Be exalted in me today, King of Glory. In Jesus' name I pray. Amen.

First, I'd like you to make a list of ancestral sins and iniquities. These would be the sins, unhealthy or unholy tendencies, sicknesses and diseases of your father and mother, their fathers and mothers, and so on into past generations. Number each one so that it will be easier for you to keep your place when you pray and renounce them later.

As we learned in chapter 4, the enemy often moves from one generation to the next. Unlike us, demons don't die. They will build a foundation of iniquity in one generation from which they will attempt to destroy the generations that follow.

Make a list of any sins or weaknesses you know of in your parents and/or grandparents. You will know some of the family sins; you may wish to look back through your family history or talk with some elderly family members. Above all, ask the Spirit to show you anything He wants you to renounce. *The purpose here is not so much to make an all-inclusive list as to list the key facts God reveals to you.* It might include things like alcoholism or other addictions, occult involvement, temper or rage, sexual perversion, secret societies like Freemasonry (Masonic Lodge), overt crimes, abortions, moral weaknesses, etc. Also include issues like heart disease, cancer, and other debilitating/deadly sicknesses and diseases.

STEP 2: UNFORGIVENESS

We learned in chapters 5 and 6 that forgiving others is crucial to our spiritual, emotional, mental, and even our physical health. Begin a second list with any person (living or dead) toward whom you've ever harbored unforgiveness. Include those whom you have hated or resented or toward whom you've held bitterness or been indifferent.

Indifference is the opposite of love; in some ways, it's even more wicked to be indifferent toward someone than to hate him. If you hate him, at least you acknowledge his existence. If you are indifferent toward him, you do not even validate that he is alive. We are to love each other with the love of Christ, including our enemies!

As you make your list, don't skimp or hedge—honesty really is the best policy. Though this list is for your eyes only, it's extremely important to your ultimate freedom that you are truthful.

STEP 3: THE OCCULT/CULTS/FALSE RELIGIONS

Now list any occultic activities in which you've been engaged. Refer to Appendix B as you make your list. Then list any cults or false religions with which you've been involved. A list of these also can be found in Appendix B.

Again, don't shortchange yourself. Ask the Holy Spirit to speak to you, and when He does, don't second-guess what you hear. God reveals in order to heal. Whether you were seriously, casually, or curiously involved isn't the point. The point is complete disclosure; the goal is complete freedom. *List them!*

STEP 4: COMMON SINS

Your next list will include any other sins that come to mind. It's true that when God saved you He forgave these sins, and it's also true "There is therefore now no condemnation to them which are in Christ Jesus" (Romans 8:1). But remember: This list is not about real guilt (which the blood of Jesus removed) but about false guilt (satanic accusation and self-condemnation).

In making my list, I went all the way back to my child-hood. I wrote down every sin I could remember committing, everything that the Holy Spirit brought to mind.

(1) When I was five years old I stole three coins from my dad's coin collection so I could buy a candy bar. . . .

(2) I lied to my mother about . . . and so on.

As you begin making your list, you won't remember every past sin—you can't even remember all the sins you committed last week. *No problem.* Again, I'm not suggesting that you make a comprehensive list; I'm suggesting that you compile an *effective* list. Jesus has promised that the Holy Spirit will guide you into all truth.[1] The enemy harasses you *selectively;* trust the Spirit to remind you of the events Satan is linking together to build his strongholds in your subconscious mind. Sit quietly before the Lord in order to give the Spirit time to reveal them to you.

Above all, disregard the severity of your sin or the age at which you committed it. The things that give the devil place in your life today may seem so insignificant to you that you've never bothered to deal with them. Satan is shrewd; he will take advantage of the most innocuous things if it means he can hold you in bondage.

On the other hand, if, for example, you've experienced illicit sex with multiple partners, write down as many of their first names as possible. If you had drug dealers, list their names. If you've committed crimes, note them. Include subtle lies, unethical practices, hidden secrets, and immoral behavior. This will take some time—if you're like me, you'll have a size-able list! Again, it's important to leave no foothold for the enemy, because where he can maintain a *foothold*, he can build a *stronghold*.

STEP 5: CONFESS THE TRUTH ABOUT YOUR SINS

Beginning with list one and continuing through lists two, three, and four, confess *aloud* the truth about each item to God. In the case of the ancestral sins, agree with Him that your relative committed (or may have committed) the particular sin or experienced the sickness or tendency. With regard to your own sins, agree with God that you indeed committed them.

It *is* important to confess the sins individually. (Remember the laundry-bag illustration in chapter 7?) Receive God's forgiveness and cleansing by praying *aloud* in this manner:

> *Father, [name of the sin] is a sin. I confess that I have sinned against you. I am so sorry, Lord. Come and cleanse me now. Thank you for forgiving me and for cleansing me from this sin through the blood of your Son, Jesus. I accept your forgiveness today.*

Repeat this procedure with each of the sins on your list.

(Hey, if you just thought to yourself, *I'll skip over this part—I can throw them all into one prayer and save some time,* that is your logical mind at work. Remember, your spirit, not your mind, was born again. Your mind must be sanctified daily by your own choice. You must continually renew your mind[2] by taking thoughts captive[3] and putting on the mind of Christ,[4] for your natural mind is unregenerate. Face it: You've tried it your way, and you're still looking for solutions. Take the time now to do this properly, once and for all.)

STEP 6: BREAK CONTRACTS WITH THE ENEMY

At the beginning of His earthly ministry, when He was in the wilderness,[5] Jesus spoke *aloud* in response to Satan's temptations. Now it's time for *you* to speak aloud to the spirits of darkness and to break any contracts you may have made with them in your sin.

This *isn't* prayer, so don't bow your head or close your eyes. Show no reverence for the enemy. Be bold. With head up, shoulders back, and a firm voice, speak to any devils that may be listening. In the case of ancestral sin, speak aloud and break any generational bonds or soul ties that exist between you and your forefathers. (*Note:* If at any point you experience sudden dizziness, nausea, or the like, it could be an indication that God is setting you free from the influence of an evil spirit. Don't let that alarm you; simply continue to renounce the enemy until God's peace settles over you.)

Say something like this:

> *Spirits of darkness, I break all contracts and take back any ground I may have given to you in [name of the sin]. God has forgiven me, and Christ's blood has cleansed me of this sin! Right now, I sever all generational iniquity between me and my mother, and her parents all the way back to Adam. And I sever all generational iniquity between me and my father, and his parents all the way back to Adam. All unholy cords are broken. I announce to you today that I am freed from your power, and from your lies, by the blood of my Lord and Savior, Jesus Christ. You no longer have any rights to my life—get out and get away from me, in Jesus' name!*

An important step in breaking these contracts is to *ask forgiveness* from the person you've offended, and the measure of the sin often determines the measure of the confession. If you've done wrong to an individual, confess to him or her; if against a group, confess to the group. It is important that you say no more than is necessary. For example, if you've talked badly about a person or group, you should, in most cases, repent for "saying things that I shouldn't have said" rather than restating your exact words (which will only make matters worse). Take care not to hurt an innocent person with your confession. If you're uncertain about how to do this, don't do it until you have the Holy Spirit's guidance. It's always wise to seek godly counsel in such matters.

Remember, the Lord also requires that we *make restitution* for sins we have committed, things we have stolen, and debts we have refused to pay.

God will often ask us to *discard possessions* that relate to our past sins. Perhaps you have occult books, astrological jewelry, a Ouija board, tarot cards, an article of clothing, blasphemous music, wicked video games, pornography, etc. Or, from a former lover, you may have gifts, photographs, love letters, or diary/journal accounts. Ask the Lord to show you what possessions you should discard or destroy, then burn them or throw them away.[6]

If you wonder, "Can't I just give them away?" then use your common sense. Be sure that you don't give to someone else anything that might be as bad for him or her as it is for you.[7]

STEP 7: MARK OFF EACH SIN AND DESTROY EACH LIST

Mark off each item as you proceed through the list, one by one. Receive your forgiveness and proclaim your freedom! Then as a prophetic act, to symbolize and express that freedom, destroy each list just as God has completely eradicated your sins. Burn it, if it doesn't present a fire safety hazard. Better still, tear it into the tiniest possible pieces. As you destroy your lists, recognize that the spiritual contracts you'd made with the enemy by participating in those sins are also utterly destroyed.

The Greatest Secret of All

The greatest victory of all was discovering that Satan's accusation, which had been my biggest problem, had become my door to victory! You see, the lists I'd made hadn't covered *everything*—I couldn't have possibly remembered it all (and neither will you). So from time to time I would find myself walking down the street and hear the enemy's familiar accusing voice: "Remember when you were twenty-three and you did . . ."

At that point I would interrupt him and say, "Thank you for bringing that to my attention, devil. You're exactly right—I did do that." Then I would turn to my heavenly Father and pray, "Lord, I thank you that you have forgiven my sin and cleansed me." Then I would say to the enemy, "Spirit of darkness, that sin is gone. I take back any ground that I gave you when I committed that sin. I tear up any contract I made with you. You have no more advantage over me. Do you have anything more to discuss? Any other accusations to make?" Invariably, he had vanished.

Again, accusing spirits have learned that accusing me will cost them more than it will cost me. I've learned to take every satanic accusation to the cross, under the blood of Christ; every time I arrive at the cross, they disappear! It's been years since I've suffered from satanic condemnation.

Suppose you're driving down the road next week and the enemy whispers to your heart, *You're not free. Don't you remember what you did behind the barn when you were thirteen?* Jesus taught in Matthew 5:25, "Agree with your adversary quickly." Immediately and audibly your response is to be, "Yes, devil, thank you for mentioning that." Then address the Lord.

Lord Jesus, the enemy is right. I did sin against you when I [name the sin]. Thank you for forgiving and cleansing me through your blood.

Then open your eyes and speak to the enemy:

In the name of Jesus, spirits of darkness, I break all contracts I made with you when I sinned. I take back any ground I gave you. Jesus Christ is my Lord. My life is under His ownership and management, so loose me now!

STEP 8: SURRENDER EVERYTHING YOU *OWN* TO CHRIST

In what other war is victory accomplished through total surrender? Yet "if, when we were enemies, we were reconciled to God by the death of his Son, much more, being reconciled, we shall be saved by his life" (Romans 5:10). I surrendered to His great love when I was lost—an enemy of God—and He saved me. But even more than that, He appropriated to me His own victory over Satan and declared me to be an overcomer. It's as though He won the world's heavyweight championship by defeating Satan at the cross, then turned around and placed His title belt around *my* waist, raised *my* hand in the air, and announced that *I* am the world's heavyweight champion . . . an overcomer. Amazing!

Once saved from the curse of my sin (justification), I was automatically drawn to experience sanctification. I discovered that God wanted to purify me, to set me apart for His holy purpose. He does this through *lordship;* He wanted to be my Lord as well as my Savior.

For Him to be my Lord, I have to yield myself completely to Him. I lay down what I consider to be "my rights." I must realize that I am no longer my own possession but was actually bought with the highest price—the blood of Jesus. I am His property, so I surrender the ownership of "my property" to Him.

Total surrender calls for me to transfer ownership of my possessions to God. This includes, for example, my house, my furniture, my investments, my savings, my collectibles, my job, and my car. For some of us, the most difficult "possessions" to yield to the Lord are our spouse and our children. In 2 Corinthians 6:10, Paul describes himself "as having nothing, and yet possessing all things."

Do you know how much the eccentric billionaire Howard Hughes left behind when he died? All of it! Dead men own nothing. Paul teaches that we are crucified with Christ,[8] which means we will hand over the ownership of everything and trust Christ in all things.

Make a list of everything you "own," then go through it one item at a time, relinquishing the ownership of every possession to God. As you do, pray *aloud* something like this:

> *Lord, from this day forward [name the item or person] belongs to you. Do with [name the item or person] whatever brings you the greatest glory and honor. Lord, all that I am and everything that I possess belongs to you. Glorify yourself in and through me.*

STEP 9: SURRENDER EVERYTHING YOU *ARE* TO CHRIST

Not only did I give my *possessions* to God, but I also gave Him my *positions*—the roles I fill. I am a husband, a father, a grandfather, an employer, a friend, a minister, a son, a brother, and so on. On that glorious day, I gave all these roles to Jesus. I admitted to Him that I was ill-equipped to be a husband, I was less than successful as a father, I wasn't the minister some folks thought I was, etc.

I remember specifically giving Him the role of being my mother's son. You see, my dear mother and I had such similar personalities that we were like fuel and fire. When we were together, we constantly discussed (some would say "argued") issues about which we disagreed. We had debated for years, and though we adored each other, our relationship wouldn't have been characterized as peaceful.

The day I relinquished my role as "my mother's son," I discovered something remarkable: God had been waiting for me to give Him the opportunity to relate to her through me. The next time she called, I actually said under my breath, "Jesus, I've given this job to you. You relate to her."

As I spoke to her on the phone, I could sense the conversation moving toward conflicting opinions. When it did, I discovered myself saying, "Well, Mother, I can certainly understand why you feel that way [although it was totally contrary to the way I felt]. I just want you to know how special you are to me and how much I love you."

At first the words were difficult to say, and I could tell they were difficult for her to hear. But as the months passed and the calls and visits occurred, I literally noticed a change in my mother. My life commitment and follow-through was actually transforming her as well as me. In fact, the last ten years of her life were delightful for both of us. I had the honor of participating in her funeral service. What a precious saint she was!

Like me, you hold various positions: husband or wife, father or mother, son or daughter, brother or sister, aunt or uncle, employer or employee, neighbor, church member, Sunday school teacher, choir member, deacon, and others. *Give Jesus every position you now hold.*

> *I am crucified with Christ: nevertheless I live; yet not I, but Christ liveth in me: and the life which I now live in the flesh I live by the faith of the Son of God, who loved me, and gave himself for me.* (Galatians 2:20)

DEAD PEOPLE NEITHER OWN POSSESSIONS NOR HOLD POSITIONS

Now proceed through this list *aloud* and ask Christ to be all that you have been trying to be:

Lord, you be [name the position] in my place. I have tried long enough to fill this role. From this moment on, I choose to let you do so. In the future, when there is an action to take, a decision to make, or a word to be spoken, you do it. Jesus, live your life through me.

Remember: Total surrender requires that you surrender *yourself* to Him—all that you are. Confess this to Him now.

My dear friend (now with the Lord) Dr. Bill Bright of Campus Crusade for Christ, taught us that within each of our hearts there is a cross and a throne. Either Christ is on the cross and self is on the throne or self is on the cross and Christ is on the throne.

The apostle Paul said, "I die daily."[9] So every morning I begin my day by surrendering my body, soul, and spirit; my mind, will, and emotions to Christ. I crown Him Lord of my life and invite Him to assume His rightful place on my heart's throne. Me? I choose to be crucified—dead to self—in order that He might live in me.

STEP 10: CONFESS THE LORDSHIP OF CHRIST

Finally, as you walk in obedience to the Lord and in the forgiveness of your sins, by faith make this threefold confession each day:

I am crucified with Christ.
Jesus, you are Lord of my life.
I am filled with Christ's Holy Spirit!

THE COUNTY FAIR

Many years ago Alice and I visited a rural East Texas county fair. One of the events that interested me most involved a flagpole. Early that morning an enterprising young man had climbed the pole and attached a $100 bill to the top, then rubbed the entire flagpole with axle grease. From there, he announced that for $1 per try, anyone could attempt to climb the pole and retrieve the $100 bill.

To the crowd's delight, one cowboy after another tried to conquer the greased pole. Each could climb only part way up; then, no matter how hard he held on, he would gradually slide back to the ground in defeat. As the day dragged on and the climbers became more inebriated, it became a hilarious sideshow. By the end of the day we never saw anyone even get close.

What I have shared with you are the steps I took to effectively "grease the flagpole of my life." No longer do I condemn myself for past failures. They are eradicated by the blood of Christ. What God cannot see will not worry me. I need not justify myself. I am justified by Christ's blood, and He has become my righteousness.

The enemy no longer has anything to gain by taunting me with false accusations. His attacks against me have become the very things that bring about his defeat in me. I now *know* and *experience* the truth, and this victory can also be yours today. May God bless you as you walk into all the freedom that Christ died to provide for you.

Father, in the name of Jesus, I ask your presence to come and fill your child, my friend, right now. Reveal to heal. Uncover and restore. Bring victory and freedom. May you come as a shield and defender to fight life's battles today. In Jesus' name, I pray. Amen.

How to Be Born Again

YOU MAY NEED A HEART TRANSPLANT

When I was a young traveling evangelist in December 1967, on a cold Sunday night, I had finished the crusade service, enjoyed dinner, and was snuggled warmly in my motel bed watching the late evening news, when I heard a startling announcement. South African surgeon (and preacher's son) Dr. Christiaan Barnard had performed the world's first human heart transplant. He'd placed the heart of Denise Darvall, a woman in her mid–twenties, fatally injured in an automobile accident, inside the chest of fifty-five-year-old diabetic Louis Washkansky, who had incurable heart disease. The new heart was actually beating on its own! That, my friend, was amazing.

When the interviewer asked Dr. Barnard why he had decided to perform such a risky operation, his answer caused me to bolt upright in bed: "One look at Mr. Washkansky, and

I knew he couldn't live with that old heart." Tears immediately flooded my eyes as I realized that I too couldn't have lived with my old heart. If you've never had one, you also need a heart transplant. Not a physical heart transplant, but a spiritual one.

The Word of God tells us, "The heart is deceitful above all things, and desperately wicked" (Jeremiah 17:9). It says that "all (of us) have sinned, and come short of the glory of God" (Romans 3:23). This means that we all have "spiritual heart disease" that is always fatal, for "the wages of sin is death" (Romans 6:23). This means spiritual death, separation from God, *in this life and for eternity.*

We're beyond the need of a spiritual heart massage—only a new heart will do. *Everyone needs a new heart.*

Good news! God loves you; He wants you to experience peace and eternal, abundant life. Today He says to you, "A new heart also will I give you . . . and I will take away the stony heart out of your flesh" (Ezekiel 36:26). The heavenly Father wants to perform the transplant you need. You cannot pay for the operation because Jesus Christ has already paid the price when He died for your sins and mine on the cross. Today you can have a new heart, a clean heart, a pure heart by doing just as David the psalmist did. He asked God for it: "Create in me a clean heart, O God" (Psalm 51:10). And guess what—the Lord did!

God didn't create us robots to automatically obey and serve Him. He created us in his own image and gave us freedom to choose for or against Him.

Like the first man and woman, Adam and Eve, who chose their own way in the Garden of Eden and sinned against God, we too have chosen to disobey Him and go our own way. The result is that our sin separates us from God.

Worse still, as hard as we may try, and regardless of our good intentions, there is no way we can be reconciled to God

apart from Jesus Christ. Only Christ and His cross can recon-
nect us to God.

Jesus died on the cross and arose from the grave in order
to pay the penalty for our sin and bridge the gap between God
and us.

Here is the solution:

(1) Recognize and admit that you've sinned against God.
(2) Acknowledge that you need a Savior, that you cannot save yourself.
(3) Repent by turning from your sins.
(4) Believe in your heart that Jesus died for you and that
the Father raised Him from the dead on the third
day. He is alive!
(5) Now trust Jesus Christ as your personal Lord and
Savior by inviting Him to live in your heart through
His Holy Spirit.

Are you ready? Good!

Right now, right where you are, turn to God and say,

*Dear God, I know that I have sinned against you. I am a
sinner. I need your forgiveness. I need a new, clean heart. I am
turning from my sins. Forgive and cleanse me. I trust you as
my Savior and give my life to you. Come into my heart today,
Risen Christ, and be Lord of my life. I choose to follow you.
Thank you for the new life you've given me. Thank you for my
new, clean heart. In Jesus' name I pray. Amen.*

Did you sincerely turn to Christ? Did you invite Him into
your life? Then congratulations! He has washed away your sins
and now lives in you! This is what the Scripture calls *being
born again,* a supernatural work of God's Spirit, who is now
within you.

This is the only cure for spiritual heart trouble. Now, with Jesus Christ as your Savior and with the new heart He has given you, you have everlasting life! Now you can relate to Him on a brand-new level. He is your Father, and you are his child. Best of all, when you take your last breath and pass from this physical body, you'll be present with God in heaven and will live with Him forever!

> *Blessed are the pure in heart: for they shall see God.*
> (Matthew 5:8)

> *The LORD seeth not as man seeth; for man looketh on the outward appearance, but the LORD looketh on the heart.*
> (1 Samuel 16:7)

Here are some helpful steps you can take to develop and deepen your new relationship with God.

(1) Get to know the Lord by reading your Bible every day. I suggest you start with the New Testament book of Philippians.

(2) Converse with God continually through prayer. Talk with Him. He is your Father now. Tell Him how you feel and what you need.

(3) Don't let sins pile up and rob you of your joy. Make a practice of confessing your sins on a daily basis.

(4) Above all, listen to Him. He will speak to your heart through His Spirit.

(5) Attend a Bible-teaching church where you can worship and serve God and fellowship with other believers.

(6) Ask the pastor to baptize you, as Jesus has commanded each of us. Water baptism is a symbol of putting off your old life in sin and putting on your

new life in Christ, a picture of burial and resurrection.

(7) Share your new life with others. Invite them to do as you have done, so they too can experience God's peace and live forever with Him.

Cults, the Occult, and False Religions

I have noticed something since Alice and I wrote *Spiritual Housecleaning: Protect Your Home and Family From Spiritual Pollution* (in which we challenged readers to recognize and renounce evil). It seems there are people in the ditches on either side of this road we call the Christian life.

In the left ditch are Christians who basically deny the presence and power of the devil. To them evil is an attitude, and Satan is little more than an intellectual concept with which, even if he is a real entity, we should not concern ourselves.

In the right ditch are Christians who seem obsessed with superstition and darkness. Some give far more time and attention to the devil and what they assume he is doing than they do to who their heavenly Father is and what He is doing.

I challenge you to take the high ground. Stay in the

middle of the road; there you are *aware* of the reality of darkness but choose to *focus* on and walk in the light. [1]

The lists of evil (below) are not exhaustive. Why?

(1) *Because any list I could compile would be obsolete in a week.* Evil, like a chameleon, continually changes colors and forms in order to deceive. There are tens of thousands of false religions and cults around the world. While many people are devoted to ancient religions, others are devoted to religions that didn't exist six months ago.

(2) *Because you need not depend upon my list.* The Holy Spirit, who lives in you, has been given to guide you into all truth. [2] I want you to learn to rely on Him and the Scriptures.

The U.S. Treasury Department doesn't train its agents to spot fake bills by immersing them in a study of counterfeiting—it teaches them to spot *real* currency. Agents will know so much about genuine currency that they will immediately recognize a counterfeit bill when they see one. Your job is not so much to be able to quickly recognize the occult but to know the truth of God so well that when it is absent, you know it!

(3) *Because such things don't merit having attention drawn to them.*

> *Have nothing to do with the barren unprofitable deeds of darkness, but, instead of that, set your faces against them; for the things which are done by these people in secret it is disgraceful even to speak of.* (Ephesians 5:11–12 WNT)

There will be times in your walk with God when you *must* draw aside and pay attention to the evil that is affecting your life and your home. Nevertheless, that will be temporary, primarily to purify yourself or to prepare for warfare prayer. Otherwise, Christ alone should be your focus! "I desire you to be truly wise as to good, but simple toward evil" (Romans 16:19 LITV).

To be sure, some Christians are called of God to study these things, but they do so with His direction and according to His will.

(4) *Because I'm not going to do your research for you.* If you want to know more about an issue, all you need is a computer connected to the Internet. If you don't have one, go to your local library. Use a search engine like *www.google.com*, and key in the element of interest. Believe me, you will be quickly overwhelmed with information.

One lady called to ask me why I disapprove of Pokemon™ (the children's game and its accompanying accessories), and I told her to search it out online. She was amazed that by following the instructions I just listed, within two seconds she had the option to browse through over eight million sites with references to Pokemon. She wouldn't finish that in a lifetime, but it doesn't usually take more than a glance at a few sites to identify an occult connection.

HOW TO IDENTIFY A CULT

(1) A cult is an individual or group that recommends or requires that you bow your knee to anyone or anything other than the Lord Jesus Christ. There is one God, and only one. [3]

(2) A cult is an individual or group that proposes any other way to God than through Jesus Christ. [4]

(3) A cult is an individual or group that suggests any other solution for your sin than the blood of Jesus. "[There is] one Priest-Mediator between God and us—Jesus, who offered himself in exchange for everyone held captive by sin, to set them all free." [5]

(4) A cult is an individual or group that says your eternal salvation is provided in any other way than through the death, burial, and resurrection of Christ. [6]

(5) A cult is an individual or group recommending that you add anything (any work of your own) to Christ's death, burial, and resurrection in order to be saved. [7]

(6) A cult is an individual or group that offers you spiritual rules or regulations other than those God clearly teaches.

> *The Spirit makes it clear that as time goes on, some are going to give up on the faith and chase after demonic illusions put forth by professional liars. These liars have lied so well and for so long that they've lost their capacity for truth. They will tell you not to get married. They'll tell you not to eat this or that food—perfectly good food God created to be eaten heartily and with thanksgiving by Christians! Everything God created is good, and to be received with thanks. Nothing is to be sneered at and thrown out. God's Word and our prayers make every item in creation holy.*
>
> *You've been raised on the Message of the faith and have followed sound teaching. Now pass on this counsel to the Christians there, and you'll be a good servant of Jesus.*
> (1 Timothy 4:1–6 THE MESSAGE)

(7) A cult is an individual or group with any philosophy or activity that refers to accessing or relying on forces, spirits, powers, energies, etc., other than the Holy Spirit. Or, anything that offers you spiritual enlightenment apart from God's Word. [8]

Example: On a Reiki Web site promoting occult healing, I find: "Reiki is one of the few healing modalities that is used for self-healing and for the healing of others. In Reiki, students receive *'attunements'* which *empower* them to do Reiki. The attunement is a *spiritual process* where *healing energy* is *activated* and *enhanced*." [9] From one sentence I have italicized six terms that in this context should be red flags to those seeking the truth.

(8) A cult is an individual or group insisting on absolute loyalty to an individual or group. True people of God will insist that you trust Him alone and that you totally commit yourself to the lordship of Jesus Christ.

Having offered these qualifications, the following lists include *examples* of what you should avoid. If you don't recognize something on these lists, don't worry. Concern yourself with those things with which you *have* been involved. Perhaps you were connected with a cult or occult items not mentioned here; in that case, follow the Holy Spirit's leading according to the peace He gives in Christ Jesus.[10]

CULTIC ACTIVITIES AND ORGANIZATIONS[11]

Astrology
Aum Shinrikyo
Baha'i Faith
Brahamism
Buddhism
Channeling
Children of God (Family of Love)
Christian Science
Church of Christ Scientist
Church Universal and Triumphant (The Summit Lighthouse)
Cybele (or Sophia)
Eastern Lightning[12]
Eckankar
Edgar Cayce
EST
Falun Gong
Fortune-Telling
Freemasonry
Feng Shui

Geomancy
Goddess Worship
Hinduism
Holism
Holy Alamo Christian Church
International Society for Krishna Consciousness (ISKCON, Hare Krishna)
Islam
    Black Panthers
    Nation of Islam
    Shiites
    Sufis
    Sunnis
    Wahhabis
Jainism
Jeanne Dixon
Jehovah's Witnesses (Watchtower)
Kabbalah
Ku Klux Klan
Lifespring Education International
Manson Cult (Charles)
Magic[13]
Martial Arts
Marxism
Mediumism
Mind Sciences
Mormonism
Native-American Religions[14]
Neo-Paganism
New Age Cults
Nostradamus
Palm-Reading
Raelian Movement
Rajneeshism

Rastafarianism

Rebirthing

Reincarnation

Reorganized Church of Jesus Christ of Latter-Day Saints[15]

Rosicrucianism

Santeria (Macumba)

Satanism

Scientology

Shamanism

Shinto

Shouters, The[16]

Sikhism

Silva Mind Control (Silva Method)

Sorcery

Spiritism

Superstition

Taoism

Tea-Leaf Reading

Telepathy

Theosophy

Transcendental Meditation

UFO Cults

Unification Church (Moonies)[17]

Unitarian-Universalist Association

Unity School of Christianity

Urantia

Vampirism

Voodoo

Water Witching

Way International, The

Wicca

Witchcraft

Witch Doctor

Yoga

Zen

Zoroastrianism

OCCULT ITEMS/ELEMENTS

- *Amulet*

  A charm used to ward off disease or evil spells.

- *Book of Mormon*

  The writings of Joseph Smith.

- *Crystal Ball*

  A high-quality, clear, colorless glass sphere used by mediums in attempts to portend the future.

- *Dragon*

  A spiritual entity described as a gigantic reptile having the claws of a lion, the tail of a serpent, wings and scaly skin; a symbol of Satan.

- *Dungeons and Dragons*

  An occult game, with many variations. (It doesn't take a rocket scientist to identify the ones that elevate darkness!)

- *Egyptian Ankh*

  A cross with a loop on top; represents a sex goddess who despises virginity; also a symbol for promoting fertility rights, worshiping Ra the Egyptian sun god (Lucifer).

- *Fetish*

  An object used to vex the environment with alleged magical powers.

- *Freemasonry*

  Items and activities related to the Masonic Order; Demolay, Eastern Star.

- *Gargoyles*

  Grotesque ornamental figures (architectural) found on old buildings; they were believed to ward off evil spirits.

- *Geomancy*

  An Asian system of designing and arranging one's life (and environs) according to a blending of geometry and spiritism, involving some of the theories of Freemasonry. (Also known as Feng Shui.)

- *Harry Potter Books*

  And other books (even children's books) encouraging occult activity.

- *I-Ching*

  Chinese fortune-telling

- *Koran*

  Or Qur'an; the writings of Muhammad, developed in 610 A.D. in what is now Saudi Arabia.

- *Obelisk*

  A tall, four-sided shaft with a pyramid-shaped point. It first appeared in the form of the Asherah pole, used in the worship of Baal and forbidden by God in the Old Testament. It was Asherah (or obelisk) that so infuriated God that He revealed himself as jealous.[18] *Asherah* comes from the Hebrew word *asher,* which means "to erect"; it is a symbol of the male phallus that refers to the earth's copulating with the sun. The obelisk is a favorite marking stone of Freemasonry—the Washington Monument, completed in 1884 and the tallest masonry structure in the world, is the most recognizable obelisk in the United States.

- *Ouija Board*™

  Also known as the witch's board. Used for communicating with spirits (demons).

- *Parapsychology*

  The study of the evidence for psychological phenomena (such as telepathy, clairvoyance, and psychokinesis) that are inexplicable to science.

- *Pentagram*

  A five-pointed star used as a magic symbol.

- *Poltergeist*

  The movement of physical objects by spirits (demons).

- *Pokemon*™

  "Pocket monsters," a devilish children's game.

- *Qigong*

  Occult healing (Chinese).

- *Rod and Pendulum*

  Tools for communicating with spirits (demons).

- *Rosary Beads*

  A string of beads used for counting prayers in Catholicism; similar prayer beads are also used by other religious groups.

- *Talisman*

  An object or charm believed to confer supernatural powers, good luck, or protection on its wearer.

- *Tarot Cards*

  A set of twenty-two playing cards consisting of a joker plus twenty-one cards depicting vices, virtues, and elemental forces; used in fortune-telling.

- *Worry Beads*

  A string of beads that the wearer fingers as a form of relaxation or distraction.

- *Zodiac*

  A celestial chart representing the paths of the principal planets of our solar system; it is the basis of astrology and is not related to the legitimate study of astronomy. Bottom line: The zodiac has nothing at all to do with the actual positions of the stars and planets.

ENDNOTES

Chapter One
1. Adapted from CompuServe News, Feb. 5, 2003.
2. Romans 10:9–10, 13.
3. 1 John 5:11.
4. Jude 1:7; see also 1 John 5:13.
5. Matthew 25:41.
6. John 8:44.
7. Revelation 4:11.
8. Jude 19; Romans 8:9.
9. John 14:2–4; Hebrews 11:16.
10. 1 Corinthians 3:1.
11. Ephesians 5:18.
12. 1 Corinthians 12.
13. Philippians 2:13.
14. Revelation 4:11.
15. 1 Corinthians 10:31; Revelation 14:7.
16. Colossians 1:27.
17. John 3:30; 2 Corinthians 12:9.
18. Galatians 2:20.
19. Colossians 3:4.
20. Ibid.

21. See Ephesians 5:8 AMP.
22. Colossians 2:10.
23. Romans 6:4.
24. Ephesians 1:4.
25. John 15:4, 7; 1 John 2:6; 3:6.
26. 2 Corinthians 5:17.
27. Ephesians 6:16.
28. 1 Corinthians 15:31.

Chapter Two

1. Isaiah 14:14.
2. Galatians 6:14.
3. 2 Timothy 2:22.
4. 1 Corinthians 2:16.
5. 2 Timothy 2:22.
6. I didn't need to know the particulars of Joan's dream in order to help her. See Ephesians 5:12.
7. See 2 Corinthians 11:14.
8. Ephesians 6:12; Revelation 12:9.
9. John 8:44.
10. See Matthew 4.
11. See Luke 2:46–47.
12. Paul E. Holdcraft, *Cyclopedia of Bible Illustrations* (New York: Abingdon-Cokesbury, 1957), 258.

Chapter Three

1. This story is adapted from our book *Spiritual Housecleaning* (Ventura, Calif.: Regal, 2003), also available at *www.prayerbookstore.com*.
2. See Ruth 4.
3. See Ruth 2.
4. Matthew 15:22–26.
5. Hebrews 5:14.
6. See Judges 3:1–3.

7. Matthew 11:12.
8. John 8:32.

Chapter Four

1. See Exodus 20:5; 34:14; Deuteronomy 4:24; et al.
2. See also Appendix B.
3. Romans 6:12–16.
4. Recorded in John 9.
5. See Lamentations 1:2, 10.
6. See John 10:10.
7. Interview: *ET* (Entertainment Tonight), July 2003.
8. See Lamentations 1:1.
9. Romans 12:1–2.

Chapter Five

1. Luke 23:40–43.
2. John 8:3–7.
3. Luke 23:34 NIV.
4. 2 Corinthians 5:19.
5. "Bob Hope's Secrets for a Long Life," *What's New,* CompuServe, July 30, 2003.
6. See James 4:17.
7. See 1 John 5.
8. See 1 Timothy 5:20.
9. Proverbs 3:5.

Chapter Six

1. *Reuters News Service,* Mar. 5, 2000, Mar. 7, 2000.
2. See James 4:17.
3. See 1 John 1:9.
4. See Matthew 3:10 and Luke 10:19.
5. See John 3:16.
6. Mark Andrew Ritchie, *Spirit of the Rain Forest* (Chicago: Island Lake Press, 1996).
7. Author unknown (edited).

Chapter Seven

1. See Genesis 18–19; Romans 1:26–27; and Galatians 5:19; 21.
2. See Hebrews 9:27.
3. John 1:29.
4. See Hebrews 9:12.

Chapter Eight

1. See Luke 7:11–17.
2. John 11:1–45, selectively paraphrased.
3. Ephesians 2:1.
4. Colossians 2:13.
5. See Ephesians 5:8.
6. See Mark 16:9.
7. See 1 John 1:9.
8. See 2 Corinthians 10:5.
9. Psalm 103.
10. See 2 Corinthians 5:17.
11. See Hebrews 10:10, 14.

Chapter Nine

1. See Matthew 5:23–24.

Chapter Ten

1. See John 16:13.
2. Romans 12:1–2.
3. 2 Corinthians 10:5.
4. 1 Corinthians 2:16.
5. See Matthew 4.
6. See Acts 19.
7. Once you've completed this book, I encourage you to read *Spiritual Housecleaning,* which addresses this issue in detail. You can find it at *www.prayerbookstore.com.*
8. Galatians 2:20.
9. 1 Corinthians 15:31.

Appendix B

1. See 1 John 1:7.
2. See John 16:13.
3. See 1 Timothy 2:5.
4. See John 14:6.
5. 1 Timothy 2:5b–6 THE MESSAGE.
6. See John 11:25.
7. See 2 Corinthians 11:4.
8. See Psalm 119:105.
9. *www.inner-sanctum.com/Reiki%20Classes.htm.*
10. Colossians 3:15.
11. Cults (for example, Mormonism and Eckankar) technically are classified separately from anti-Christian world religions (for example, Islam and Hinduism); for the purposes of this book, however, they are categorized together.
12. An offshoot of the Witness Lee Local Church in China.
13. Black Magic, White Magic. Not sleight-of-hand, mechanical stage entertainment, but spiritual magic that actually seeks to access the power of spirits or demons.
14. Some of the belief systems, not all.
15. Offshoot of Mormonism.
16. Offshoot of the Witness Lee Local Church in China.
17. Followers of Korean Reverend Sun Myung Moon.
18. See Exodus 34:13–14; 1 Kings 14:15; 15:13.

INDEX

HOW TO CONTACT
EDDIE AND ALICE SMITH

Author, speaker, preacher Eddie Smith, and his wife, Alice, travel worldwide teaching on various themes related to prayer and discipleship.

The Smiths teach together as well as individually.

For information about hosting the Smiths for a conference in your church or city, submit your online invitation at: *www.usprayercenter.org*.

Prayer Resources

Eddie and Alice Smith's books and materials, as well as other resources they recommend, can be found at: *www.prayerbookstore.com*.

Free Newsletter

Join thousands worldwide who receive the PrayerNet Newsletter, Eddie and Alice's FREE biweekly informative e-mail publication. Subscribe at: *www.usprayercenter.org*.

Eddie Smith
U.S. PRAYER CENTER
7710-T Cherry Park Dr., Ste. 224
Houston, TX 77095
Phone: (713) 466-4009 FAX: (713) 466-5633
E-mail: usprayercenter@cs.com
Web site: *www.usprayercenter.org*
Resource Center: *www.prayerbookstore.com*